6 | 1)

EssexWorks.

For a better quality of life

FIN

Please return this book on or before the date shown above. To renew go to www.essex.gov.uk/libraries, ring 0845 603 7628 or go to any Essex library.

ex County Council

D0185921

JOHN WILSON'S
FISHING TIPS

JOHN WILSON'S
FISHING TIPS

First published in the UK in 2012

© Demand Media Limited 2012

www.demand-media.co.uk

Printed and bound in China

ISBN 978-1-909217-02-7

Contents

Barbel

1 To stop chub from hooking themselves and disturbing the swim when barbel fishing with 'bolt-rig' style tactics, use a 12 inch hook length and a long (1-2 inch) hair, in conjunction with a heavy 2-3 ounce 'running' flat-bomb. Use a rubber cushioning bead between hook trace swivel and lead. They will then freely move away across the current or turn immediately downstream with the lower of your two 15-18mm boilies, large boilie or halibut pellet pursed in their lips, but usually spit it out at the last second. So only lift into a fish when the rod tip slams round and stays round, indicating a barbel has found the bait. Ignore all other pulls.

2 Have you ever wondered why a 'sand-papery' feeling happens to the line when you are touch ledgering for barbel, or the rod tip vibrates momentarily before 'hooping over' as a fish runs off with the bait and actually hooks itself? Well, as barbel are equipped with four long sensory barbels (hence their name) an under-slung mouth and a long snout, unlike fish such as chub, roach and tench, they actually lose visual contact with what they are about to swallow before opening their mouth. So they gently move their snout from side to side in an agitated manner, in order to centralize the bait once their mouth is open. And in so doing, their barbels must inevitably do a 'plink-

Above: Tip 2

plunk' against the line.

3 When baiting up a swim, either loose feeding by hand from a spot several yards upstream to allow for the pace of flow to ensure the food is deposited exactly where you want it on the river bed, or by using bait droppers full of maggots, hempseed or 3-6mm pellets, possibly the three most effective attractor 'loose feeds' for barbel, try not to fish immediately afterwards. Action is invariably more hectic and lasts for much longer if you first allow the barbel to move into the swim and over the bait, gaining confidence in their feeding, for at least an hour or so, before your hook rig is presented to them. Try it and see.

4 During the warm summer and autumnal months barbel are far more likely to move across the flow and intercept a moving bait, even one being 'trotted' through at current speed, than later on in the year when temperatures start to plummet, and they will only suck up static baits from the bottom. So get to enjoy catching some barbel on the float, using a powerful 13 foot trotting rod and centre pin reel holding 6-8lbs test. Keep a selection of both heavy 'Avon' and 'Chubber' floats in your waistcoat, and be sure to split their bulk shotting capacity of say 3-5 swan shots, into a line of AAs fixed onto the line 12-16 inches above the hook, with a small shot or two in between. See Grayling Tip 1.

Above: Tip 5

5 To get the most out of your river, especially when exploring those barbel-holding runs beneath willows and lines of alders along the opposite bank (I bet certain, previously unattainable swims immediately spring to mind here) you need to get in with the fish, at least into the centre of the river, in order to trot a bait through steadily and directly downstream. This means splashing out on a pair of lightweight, chest-high, waders. The best are 'breathable' and come with hard-wearing neoprene reinforcement at the knees and built-in neoprene socks. You then simply slip on 'felt-soled' wading shoes for maximum stability over slippery stones and boulders. Anyone who fly fishes for salmon or sea trout or who long trots for grayling during the winter months,

will no doubt be equipped already. Either way, quality chest-high waders are a sound investment for enjoyment, allowing you to also kneel and sit down on the bank anywhere along the river without the need for a stool.

6 When ledgering at close range 'bolt-rig' style for barbel (or carp) in really clear water where they can be viewed moving all around the bait to inspect it, even above your ledger rig, it pays to incorporate a 'back-lead' positioned on the line two to four foot above the bait. Simply and 'loosely' pinch onto the line two 3x swan shots, or sleeve a coffin ledger onto the line and secure with a rubber 'sliding float stop' at each end. This ensures that the line above your ledger rig is ironed flat to the river bed, thus alleviating any chance of lines bites and fish spooking through their fins touching the line, It is especially important when having to fish from 'high-bank' swims, where the line would otherwise angle down sharply from rod tip to ledger rig.

7 If like me you welcome the rest provided by the statutory closed season for rivers, but after a few weeks start to get itchy to be beside water, why not pay your favourite 'barbel' stretches

a visit. From around the beginning of May onwards (depending upon water temperatures) barbel congregate upon the gravel shallows in readiness for spawning, and so there is no better time for 'fish-spotting', and ascertaining to exactly what size they grow along a particular part of the river. So don't forget the Polaroid glasses.

8 When clear-water barbel do not play ball and move up into a pre-baited swim, pushing smaller fish species out of the way, as they usually do, then plan to fish for them during the hours of darkness. This reluctance to feed aggressively during daylight hours is common place in stretches of river where the barbel are targeted daily, particularly with small groups of 'known' or 'specimen-sized fish' that have been repeatedly caught and know all the tricks. So plan to start an hour or so before dusk, expecting no small level of response once the light has totally gone, and be prepared to fish on for some while until they do respond. Those first few hours of darkness are usually best. But don't forget a trip during that first hour or two before dawn, which can so often produce, especially during the warmer months.

Above: Tip 6

9 For depositing any kind of loose feed straight down to the river bed of close range swims (say up to a rod length and a half out) regardless of current force, bait droppers, which come in all shapes and sizes, are worth their weight in gold. Monster droppers holding half a pint of hempseed, maggots or pellets etc, get the job done in no time at all and minimize disturbance, though you do need a long, stiff rod to swing a large 'full' dropper out. And droppers must be 'swung' out and not 'cast', otherwise bait could get distributed all over the place. And you want it concentrated within a relatively small area over which the barbel will eventually move and start hoovering it up. Beware of the odd pike which appear from nowhere to attack the lid of the dropper when it hangs down and 'flaps' in the current as you lift it out.

BARBEL

Right: Tip 12

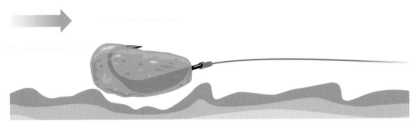

10 One of the most satisfying and pleasing techniques for catching barbel occurs during the warmer months when donning chest-high waders and getting into clear-flowing, gravel-bottomed rivers allows you to carefully wade out to a position immediately below a shoal of fish, (which can often be seen hugging the bottom in the runs between long beds of flowing weed) and then to cast a chunk of luncheon meat upstream and slightly across, so it rolls back along the bottom directly in line with the shoal. And to do this you must allow an all-important 'bow' to form in the line between rod tip and bait.

11 'Rolling meat', as the method has been dubbed, works effectively for one main reason. The free lined bait is brought down to the shoal at current speed, like all loose particles of natural food, so their suspicion is not aroused, and moreover, it comes 'directly' down river, tumbling along the gravel, and is not dragged 'unnaturally' across the fish's vision which is what the line would do if you were situated on the bank and not standing in the water immediately downriver.

12 To facilitate easy casting and to counteract the bait's inherent buoyancy when 'rolling meat' so it tumbles along naturally, catching momentarily here and there every so often amongst the clean gravel, just like all other tit bits brought along by the current, a slither of lead wire (roofing lead is exactly the right thickness) is super-glued to the top of the hook shank and firmly whipped over with black fly

tying thread. Chamfering each end of the lead with your thumbnail makes for an extremely neat finish. See Diagram. The hook now looking decidedly 'shrimp-like' with its 'curved' back, will always present the bait with the hook point angled upwards, and is thus less likely to catch upon snags or weed. Generally however, large chunks of meat are used in order that the hook is not actually visible.

13 You can make up several different 'weights' of hooks, (to cover all conditions from slow currents to turbulent runs) simply by using different thicknesses of lead wire. I suggest large sizes of 'wide gape' eyed hooks from 6 up to 2 will serve you best. And in addition to luncheon meat, tinned ham, sausage in skins, etc, etc, even good old bread flake and protein pastes will all make this method work and come alive.

14 For extra sensitivity when 'rolling meat', a braided reel line used in conjunction with a free running centre-pin reel is hard to beat, though you can manage with a fixed spool reel and monofilament. The secret being always to gently recover line as the bait is brought down to you by the current, whilst keeping that 'bow' in the line, which could suddenly 'tighten' or completely

fall 'slack' as a fish hoovers up the bait and belts downstream towards you.

15 When 'bolt-rig' style ledgering for barbel (and chub) particularly when the river is in full flood and visibility is at an all time low, give your bait added attraction by moulding a large dollop of soft, aromatic paste around your hair-rigged boilie or halibut pellet. As pieces break off or are pecked off by small fish and roll downstream, barbel will follow the scent up to your hook bait.

16 When smaller specimens pick up your ledgered size 10-15mm boilie or pellet hook bait, simply tie on

Below: Tip 16

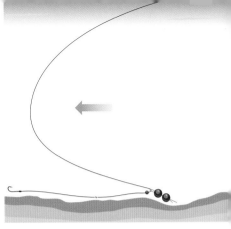

a longer hair to accommodate two size 20mm boilies or a 25mm halibut pellet. The mouth of a double figure barbel can easily hoover them up.

17 If you have your sights set on a really big barbel, remember that a September fish for instance, could weigh as much as 10-15% heavier towards the end of the season in March. So providing the weather stays mild, concentrate your efforts during those 'precious' last two weeks of the river season.

18 There's no doubt about it, barbel love maggots. Trouble is, so does every other cyprinid species, so wherever small, nuisance fish share a particular swim with barbel you must be prepared to 'feed them off'. And that means having enough

maggots to keep loose feeding till all the lesser fish are literally full up, by keeping a steady stream going through the swim, either by throwing in maggots by hand or depositing them straight down to the bottom of really fast runs through continual use of a bait dropper. In small rivers a gallon of maggots is not excessive, while in rivers twice the size, you'll need twice as many maggots. But eventually, and it may take an hour or two, those barbel will be the only fish still munching maggots. Then you could clean up. And in clear-flowing swims where the fish are plainly visible, even select a particular specimen and watch it hoover in your bunch of maggots.

19 If you're planning to catch barbel from a deep, even-

paced run close into the bank, then why not anchor your bait to the river bed using a mini link-ledger, but have a float to watch on the surface. This devastatingly effective rig is called 'stret-pegging' and allows you to watch a float (which must lie flat on the surface) due to the exaggerated subsurface bow in the line between float and link-ledger. You simply set the float, a Chubber, Avon or large Balsa, fixed with silicon tubing at both ends, at least twice the depth of the swim (keep pushing it up the line till the set-up works) and cast directly downstream. See Diagram.

20 The secret of stret-pegging, once the mini ledger (in slow swims a single swan shot is sufficient) has anchored the bait to the bottom, is in allowing a little loose line, for the subsurface 'bow' to form and the float to settle 'lying flat', before placing the rod in two rests with the tip angled up a little. The float should now be swaying gently from side to side in the current, (literally any speed water may be fished in this way so long as your float is set far enough over depth) and when a fish takes the bait, it will cock and glide positively under all in one. A lovely sight to see, not only when barbel fishing, because any bottom-feeding river fish may be caught stret-pegging. See Carp Tip 13.

21 Though float fishing, the close-in technique of stret-pegging is best executed using a 11-12 foot Avon style rod, rather than a lighter 'waggler' rod.

Bream

Above Right:
Tip 2

1 Want to catch bream on the float that are feeding over weed or amongst 'cabbages' in still or slow moving water? Then 'float ledgering' is often the answer, using a peacock quill waggler float (attached with silicon tubing around the bottom end – not locked with shot) and set a foot or two over depth. But not with a small bomb stopped several inches from the hook by a small shot. This would drag the bait and hook length into the weed and minimize bites. Far better to use a 20-30 inch (depending upon weed density and height) 'weight link', joined to the reel line 20-24 inches above the hook using a 'four-turn water knot'. And simply pinch 2-3 large swan shot onto

the end of the link. Don't worry about the float's actual shotting capacity.

2 Use buoyant baits when float-ledgering, like bread flake or crust, which will lie on top of the weed, and remember to angle the rod top upwards in a flow, in order to ensure that minimal line is on the surface, which will stop the float tip from pulling under. But when your rig is settled on the bottom, you can tighten up so that only a small part of the tip is showing. Bites are registered by the float tip simply disappearing positively, though occasionally by it rising, if a bream 'lifts' the shots from the weed. Works well for tench, and carp too.

3 Rather than wait for 'difficult to miss' slammers which rarely

Above: Tip 4

Above Left: Tip 3

materialize when quiver-tip ledgering rivers for winter bream, (summer fish are entirely different), be prepared to strike at any 'strange' movement on the tip. Keep the rod angled up high (on two rests) to alleviate excess current pressure against the reel line, and you'll find that 'just' holding bottom (and this is the secret) with a couple or three 3x swan shot, is possible in the strongest flow.

4 'Drop-back' indications are often the bites to look for when quiver-tipping for bream, where the tip suddenly and seemingly without reason, momentarily 'eases' or 'jerks' back because the shots have slightly moved due to a bream inhaling the bait. Forward pulls and vibratory pulses of the tip are also worth hitting, but those 'drop-backs' will put far more bream in your net. So juggle about with the amount of shots on your ledger link, ensuring that they only 'just' hold bottom. Anything more or less, is a bite.

5 The silver bream is in British waters extremely rare, and mainly confined to East Anglia and the Midlands. This decidedly 'delicate-looking' fish takes most small baits used for roach and rudd and prefers still and slow moving waters. It lacks the thick covering of mucus associated with common bream, and the scales are quite large and noticeably 'silvery',

hence its name. It has a small head, large eyes and less of a protrusible mouth than common bream. When erect the silver bream's dorsal fin is unusually high, and its pectoral, pelvic and anal fins (unlike the common bream) show a tinge of orangey-pink, rather similar to the dace.

6 When 'slider-float' fishing for bream in deep, still waters, always use a 'bodied-waggler' float carrying more shot than would seem necessary. This is to ensure the reel line passes freely through the float's eye or ring, quickly taking the bait down to the bottom. Bulk most of the shot (against which the float will rest for casting) 3-4 feet above the bait, with two small shots in between, the lowest positioned 6-10 inches from the hook actually resting on the bottom.

Using several inches of slightly 'finer' line, tie a five turn stop knot onto the reel line above the float at the desired depth for bait presentation, leaving both ends 1-1½ inches long, ensuring they 'fold' when passing through the rod rings. If the float's bottom ring or eye allows the stop knot to slip through, use a tiny (2-3mm) bead between it and the knot.

7 Remember always to dip the rod tip immediately after casting when slider-float fishing, and wind like crazy for a few turns, in order to ensure all the line sinks between float and rod tip to counter act any sub-surface draw, and quickly open the reel's bale arm allowing line to peel freely from the spool and eventually through the float's bottom ring till the bait touches bottom and the float cocks. Lastly, remember to strike 'sideways' in order to pull the line 'through' the water and the hook into the bream, as opposed to losing striking power by trying to 'lift' the line 'against' surface tension; which is next to impossible!

8 When distance ledgering for big, still-water bream, hitting bites is always a problem. Taking a leaf from the carp angler's book however by incorporating a mini-shock, or 'bolt rig' into your end tackle, will result in those bream actually pulling a small hook into themselves. Method feeders with internal elastic are much favoured, (which alleviates snap-offs) to which a short 4-5 inch hook length of 10lbs test soft braid is tied with a size 12 or 10 hook on the business end. As for reel line, due to the long casting of a heavy ball of bait, do not go below

8lbs test.

9 The bait for distance ledgering for bream like a 10mm boilie, pellet, or three grains of corn etc, is then hair-rigged, and immediately prior to casting a ball of 'method-mix ground bait' (to which hempseed, corn, casters and chopped worms etc, have been added) is firmly moulded around the feeder, with the hook bait carefully hidden inside.

After casting to the desired spot, (use a marker float cast out using another rod - so all the bait ends up within a relatively small area), the line is tightened up, and a heavy, 'swinger type' bite indicator clipped onto the line (on a short drop) in front of the bite alarm, so that should a bream swim towards the rod, the indicator will fall and indicate a drop-back bite.

10 When fishing the 'waggler' for bream in still water, one of the most common problems is avoiding the 'drift'. So here are three tips for beating it. Start by sloshing a finger full of washing up liquid around the line on your reel's spool, which will quickly sink the line. Second, use a really long, straight peacock waggler with a bulk shot capacity of at least four to five SSG shots so all the locking

shots are well beneath the surface and below the 'top drifting layer'. And lastly, fish over depth with one or two No 6 or 8 shots dragging along the bottom, which acts like a 'brake' to help keep the bait in position.

11 Feeder fishing for bream in still waters usually revolves around incorporating a clear plastic open-end or cage-type swim feeder made from wire mesh, into your ledger rig. A 'fixed paternoster' tied using a four turn water knot is best for this. And 'plugging' as it is often called, is the secret to this method, because you don't want feed coming out on the cast and baiting up areas you're not fishing.

Start by pressing one end of your feeder into the ground bait mix (not over-dampened) gently pressing the ground bait inside to block that end. Then put in some loose feed, sweet corn, casters, finely chopped worm etc, but leave enough room at the opposite end for another plug of ground bait. Finally, squeeze tightly at both ends using thumb and forefinger, immediately before casting, and providing you have not 'over-wetted' the ground bait, the feeder will explode its contents ONLY when it reaches the lake bottom.

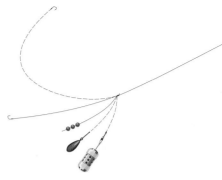

Above & Above Right: Tip 12

12 When standard ledgering or feeder fishing for bream in both still and running water, regardless of whether you use a swing tip, a quiver tip or a hanging bobbin-type indicator, a 'running' ledger is not required. The simple 'fixed paternoster' is the best rig by far, and to make one simply tie an 8-10 inch length of line (could be reel line or thicker) onto your mainline using a four turn water knot. This forms the 'link' to which shots, bomb or feeder are attached. For feeders and bombs add a tiny snap swivel to facilitate quick changing.

How far up the line from the hook you tie this link depends on whether you are presenting a 'static' bait, or are hoping to encourage bites 'on the drop'. For the latter, start with a tail of around 4-5 feet. For static baits 18-24 inches is ideal. If you wish to use a hook tail of a lighter breaking strain than your reel line, for a more natural presentation of say slowly falling baits like casters and maggots, then simply tie this, again using the four turn water knot, say 10 inches from the end of your mainline, which itself then becomes the 'ledger link'. See Diagram.

13 When ledgering in still and slow moving rivers for bream, quiver tip and bobbin-type bite indicators are not only more commonly used than the 'swing-tip', but they are more versatile. The trouble with swing tips, though unbelievably sensitive, is that they wobble about too much when trying to cast any reasonable distance, causing the mainline to wrap around the rod tip and tangle.

Swing tips do however have one redeeming feature, and that is showing the difference between line bites and true bites. 'Liners' cause the tip to twitch and jiggle about in short, sharp lifts. Whereas with true bites, the tip continues to rise until it points directly at the bream. Or, should the bream swim towards the rod, thus moving the lead or feeder, the tip simply 'falls back' dramatically. So in certain circumstances, especially for short to medium range ledgering, there is still good reason for using a swing tip indicator.

14 When feeder fishing for bream in shallow still waters, say less than six foot deep, put your faith in plastic or wire mesh 'cage-feeders' which ensure that the ground bait filling 'explodes' quickly and easily, forming an attractive cloud that doesn't spook the fish.

But you don't want this to happen if ledgering a 20 foot deep swim in Ireland's fast flowing River Shannon, where a large, open end, clear, plastic feeder will retain the bait as it sinks and release only with impact with the river bed. Remember: Fishing is 'horses for courses'.

15 If you are distance-ledgering a still water that requires constant baiting with ground bait balls, add a few drops of oil-based liquid 'additive' to your feeder mix on the next cast, to leave a 'slick' on the surface, as a target for aiming your ground bait.

16 To catch big bream on 'static' baits that are situated within pole range in both wide, deep rivers (6-20 foot plus) and smaller, deep and fast flowing rivers, consider a 'Polaris' slider float set up. The wire-stemmed 'Polaris' slides on the 4-5lbs running line (pinch a small shot at mid depth against which it rests while being shipped out) and automatically locks like magic (via the 'Frixon' device at the floats base) at the desired depth once the one ounce bomb has settled. Use a four turn water knot to attach a 12 inch hook link five inches above the bomb, and pinch on a tiny shot five inches above the hook to keep the bait anchored to the river bed.

Left: Tip 16

Below: Tip 17

17 If quiver-tip ledgering for bream in large, open waters remember that during extremely windy conditions, there will be a considerable 'subsurface tow' caused by the waves hitting one end of the lake which subsequently forces surface water down, and back up the lake. So for maximum line pick up on the strike, sit parallel to the bank actually facing wind direction, and make sweeping, sideways strikes.

18 You never know when you might be wanting to slider-float fish for bream in excessively deep still water, so always keep a few 'Polaris' floats in your box. Setting up these 'self-locking' floats is easy. Thread your reel line down through one of the two holes in the tubular 'Frixon' locking device

at the bottom, and make up a fixed paternoster end rig incorporating either a bomb or feeder rig. The small hole accommodates lines in the 3-6lbs range and the larger, heavier lines. Then pinch on a No 1 shot three feet up the line for the float to rest against when casting.

It is imperative not to use less weight in the terminal set up than is recommended, otherwise the float's buoyancy will only drag the bait along the bottom when you try to tighten up.

19 Float ledgering using a 'Polaris' is the best way of beating that eternal problem experienced when ledgering for bream line bites. But because of the enormous 'right angle' of line that exists between bait and rod tip once the float has automatically 'locked', setting large hooks at distance can prove troublesome. So use smaller hooks and smaller baits when fishing the 'Polaris' and if you do inexplicably miss bites, try winding in fast for a couple of seconds before lifting the rod into a strike. This will effectively take up that slack line.

20 Having trouble getting the specimen-sized bream of rich and clear water lakes or pits to pick up your baits during daylight hours? Then simply fish for them during darkness when they naturally feed more ravenously.

Carp

1 One of the most simplistic and, consequently, most delightful ways of catching carp (any sized carp) at close range, is fishing the 'lift-method' with 4-6 inches of peacock quill attached bottom end only with a sleeve of silicon tubing, (locking shots result in the line breaking should a carp plunge through weeds), set slightly over depth. Using a reel line of around 8-10lbs test, with a single swan shot pinched on 5-6 inches above a size 10-8 hook, completes the rig. Bait can be pellets, maize or small boilies, hair rigged, with loose feed of the same or smaller, pellets or particles. The permutations are like carp fishing itself: endless.

2 When fishing the 'lift', the rod is best supported (no rod rests are used for this technique) beneath the forearm and rested

Above: Tip 1

upon your knee, after an 'underarm–flick' cast is made several feet further out than you have introduced 'loose-feed'. This is for good reason, because you need to quickly wind the rig back (with the float well clear of the surface) so the exposed hook does not catch up on bottom debris, or the shot bump into feeding carp, before allowing it to settle on the bottom directly amongst the loose feed. Gently tighten the line so the float is 'all but cocking' and wait, whilst holding the rod throughout.

Line bites will make the float sway and jerk, almost dipping it under at times, as the tails or pectoral fins of carp momentarily catch the line. One reason why I like the float lying 'flat'. 'Lift bites' will still be recognizable however, whenever a carp 'lifts' the single shot up, by the float suddenly 'drifting' as though someone has cut the line with a pair of scissors. But most bites will consist of the float suddenly 'cocking and disappearing' all in one motion...lovely!

3 A 'marker-float' outfit is required whenever you intend distance casting to an area that has been pre-baited for carp (works for tench and bream too) using a spod or radio-controlled boat. In fact, exploring with the marker float outfit is the very first task. Use an entirely separate outfit (to your fishing rods) such as a long 12-13 foot powerful carp or pike rod, a heavy (3-5 ounce) lead and a 30-50lbs test braided reel line. Simply thread a large rubber bead onto the end of your braided line, followed by the lead (which should have a large-swivelled eye) and another bead, and tie to the bottom ring of your marker float. Be sure to use one that incorporates a large, vane-type top that can easily be seen at distance.

After making an exploratory cast, if your rod 'locks-up' as you try to drag the lead back along the bottom, then you have located a weed bed. If you feel no resistance as the lead is being wound back, then you have found a weed-free area, with the bottom consisting of sand, mud or silt. If however you feel a little 'knocking' transmitted through the rod,

your lead will be dragging over stones or a gravel bar. So select your 'fishing ground' and once the float is settled as a marker for both casting to and baiting up, sink all the line between float and rod tip by attaching a heavy 'back lead' close into the bank. With your entire marker float line now ironed to the bottom and the rod tip dunked below the surface and out of the way, you should not catch up on it throughout the session. And it can be simply wound in when you leave.

4 If you love catching carp off the top using small floating baits like mixer biscuits and floating pellets etc, here's a useful tip which allows you to quickly change from a 'floating controller' set up geared to fishing distances of up to 50 yards, to just the plain hook, for those times when fish move in ridiculously close, and you merely wish to suspend the floater directly below the rod tip, free-line style.

Start by threading onto your 8-12lbs reel line a floating controller such as a 'Tenpin', followed by a 3mm, black, rubber bead, and then tie a five turn stop knot (using a few inches of reel line) before tying on a size 10 hook direct to the reel line 2-4 feet below the Tenpin. See Diagram.

To quickly 'de-rig', simply work the rubber bead over the stop knot and all the way along the hook's shank and off the point, followed by the swivel at the top of the Tenpin. This literally takes seconds, and you are left with the bare hook. Repeat to be fishing with the controller again. Obviously, this can only be achieved when using a small 'rubber' bead. See Rudd Tip 4, for fishing 'lighter'.

5 To present small floaters to carp like mixer biscuits, sunflower seeds, floating pellets or even small boilies etc, use a small, but strong hook (a size 10 is ideal and will land the biggest carp) and so that it sits immediately 'below' the floater where it is less inhibitive to a 'taking' fish, simply cut a shallow groove in the bait using a junior hacksaw blade, and super-glue along the hook shank. Once you have mastered this technique, very rarely will a bait come off during the hardest of casts. I even glue my pellet or biscuit floaters on when 'fly-rodding' for carp using powerful 'double-haul' casting.

6 Both clear and brown-coloured latex rubber 'bait bands', most of which come with a small, built-in dimple tab at the top through which the hook point is passed, are another excellent way of quickly attaching square-shaped floaters to your hook. Being tough and flexible, they come in varying sizes to accommodate virtually any sized floater.

7 At some time or another everyone is faced with the difficult task of extracting hooked carp out of lilies. The secret if there is one, and this works for me, is to watch carefully where your line actually goes into the pads, which we'll assume for argument's sake are both thick and extensive. Because you need to get the rod tip down low for some 'side-strain' hauling, following the exact 'angle' at which the carp is heading. And continue pulling with the rod nicely bent, in that direction till it is 'hauled' back, changing direction accordingly with your angle of pull each time the carp moves

position. It is a strange but very effective technique.

Obviously you need an all-through action rod that bends in harmony with the stretch in your line for this. It's simply no good heaving away with the rod held straight up high and fully bent if the fish has gone straight into the lilies and turned sharp right, winding the line at an acute angle around a clump of stems. The torque upon your tackle is immense. But steady and continual pressure from the right angle, will surprisingly, extract the largest of fish. One reason why I endeavour only to float fish or free line when tackling 'lily-bed carp'. The less on the line in the way of rigs, leads, tubing, anti-tangle this and anti-tangle that, the better. And as my float (a few inches of peacock quill) is always attached with a sleeve of silicon tubing, it immediately comes off as a fish enters the pads, as does the large single shot lightly pinched onto the line several inches from the hook.

8 Whether ledgering for carp at close or long range, due to varying bottom contours over which your line is bound to hang, 'line bites' can at times, prove a real problem, making the carp even more wary as they approach your bait. To alleviate this simply clip a 'back-lead' to your line immediately in front of the rod tip after casting and let it slide down to the bottom, thus pinning the line down between ledger rig and rod. Remember however, that this only works when employing 'bolt-rig' tactics where due to the weight of the lead, the fish more or less hooks itself.

9 For stalking summer carp, when carrying the very minimum of tackle invariably results in more fish on the bank simply because you haven't scared the fish away from the margins, it's worth investing in a 'stalking belt'. Designed to be worn around the waist with a variety of pockets at the side and at the rear, these 'bum-bag' type belts are capable of holding scales, a compact camera, baits, plus hooks, floats, shot and rig bits etc, leaving you free, clutching just rod and net, to crawl stealthily through dense vegetation in order to creep up on the whoppers slurping amongst the tree roots.

10 When the carp inhabiting large sheets of deep still water are cruising in the warm upper layers, sometimes topping, sometimes a few feet below, seemingly aimlessly moving about, one technique that can really sort them out is the 'Zig-rig' which on a size 8 hook, is used to present a small, rectangular, hair-rigged piece of buoyant cork, about the size of a mixer biscuit (but, 'yes' cork!) at any depth from the surface to several feet down. It resembles a pop-up boilie or imitation floater like a

mixer biscuit, and is, believe it or not, readily taken.

The rig comprises of a heavy in-line, semi-fixed 3-4 ounce lead, through which the mainline passes before it is attached, via the swivel, to hook a length anything up to (assuming you are casting with 12 foot rods) 12 feet long, (you're fishing deep water remember), which means that the imitation, buoyant cork bait can be presented two feet below the surface (by far the best 'taking' distance) in a maximum of 14 foot of water. After casting, putting the rod in its rest and tightening up, hang a weighted swinger-type bobbin on the line and be ready for strange, 'drop-back' bites which sometimes just keep dropping. But do not strike yet. Wait for the fish to pull the indicator up tight before setting the hook.

A most 'versatile' variation to this set up is to use a 3-4 ounce 'running lead' with a rubber 'cushioning' bead between lead and a buoyant, plastic sub-float. To the opposite end of the sub-float tie on a two foot hook length and hair-rigged cork bait already described. Then upon the lead settling on the bottom, free line is slowly given till the sub-float and floating bait pop up to the surface. Now slowly wind till the sub-float disappears, adding just four feet of line to the reel, if you wish the cork to be presented

two feet below the surface. But it can of course be fished at any depth from two feet above bottom upwards, all the way to the surface. And there are days when it pays to experiment. So clip on an indicator and set the bite alarm.

If bites do not materialize, slowly wind the sub-float and bait down to four, six or eight feet, and so on below the surface until a 'taking' depth is found. Most fish will hook themselves whilst moving off against the buoyancy of the sub-float, and give screaming runs.

11 Here's a handy tip for presenting your bait using a 'bolt-rig' set up to carp amongst dense weed beds when you have no option. Firstly step up your reel line breaking strain accordingly, and match it to a powerful 'all-through' action rod, which collapses into a 'full bend' and absorbs all the lunges of a big carp thrashing and crashing through weed beds.

For the best presentation of your rig and bait, everything needs to be tucked away carefully into a clear PVA bag including a 2-3 ounce lead (to get you easily through the weed) plus some loose feed like small pellets etc, (secure the top of the bag using PVA string or tape, so that after casting through the weed and the bag dissolves, both hook bait and freebies are in plain view and nothing

is 'hung-up'). Lastly, don't go far from your rod. It actually needs to be to hand, in order that you can respond immediately to a bite by bending into a fish and hauling it around before it travels too far.

12 Contrary to popular belief fuelled by the hype of 'pre-made' bait manufacturers, plain old 'maggots' are one of the most effective of all baits to catch carp. Trouble is, when used in ones, twos and threes, maggots are not SELECTIVE, and just about every fish in every water, from a two inch roach upwards, love them. The answer therefore is to present a real 'mouthful' if you only want to catch larger species like carp. And a method devised exactly to this end, is the 'Korda maggot clip'. A cunning device that permits dozens of maggots to be threaded onto a fine wire ring without bursting any of them, which in turn is then attached (via a quick-change clip) to the loop of a 'hair-rig'. You can even add slithers of rig foam cut to the shape and size of maggots should you wish to present your bunch of maggots 'pop-up' style above bottom weed. Clever, isn't it?

13 With more and more carp these days making their way into British river systems from adjacent gravel pit fisheries during flood time, including some 'whoppers', do you fancy catching them on the float in running water? Well, then the technique of stret-pegging is simply unbeatable. And you don't need heavy tackle either.

Stret-pegging in rivers is a 'close-range' method, so a heavy Avon-style rod coupled to a centre pin or fixed spool reel holding 8-10lbs test monofilament is quite adequate. Fix onto the reel line several feet deeper than the swim, (with a band of silicone tubing at each end) an 8-10 inch straight waggler float, or unpainted length of peacock quill. It matters not because they are the same thing really.

Ten to 12 inches above your hook (all baits and hair-rig options are open here) pinch on a single SSG shot, and above this fold a short length of mono (could be reel line) and secure as a 'running ledger' by securing with two or three 3X SSG shot, leaving enough gap so the 'mini-ledger' can slide up the line. Now, cast the rig directly downstream over your baited area, and once the rig has touched bottom, allow a little slack for the float to come around and lay 'flat'. If it doesn't, push it further up the line

till it does lay flat.

Angle the rod on two rests with the tip pointing upwards and wait for events. From swaying gently in the current, the float will suddenly cock and slide under, all in one glorious moment. See Diagram in Barbel Tip 19.

14 Should you witness the sad sight of a freshly killed, partly eaten carp lying up on the bank or in the margins of your local fishery, (as shown in the accompanying photo here, it was unfortunately from my own two-lake fishery) then inform the owner immediately. Such devastation is caused by otters released into a river environment where due to cormorant predation upon silver shoal fishes combined with a much reduced annual run of eels, during the winter months especially, they roam far and wide (up to 10 miles from their home) to enjoy the easy pickings of carp stocked into still water lakes and pits, because the rivers are bare.

15 Contrary to popular belief, whilst otters may be perceived by the public as cute and cuddly, they are in fact indiscriminate killers, which during the warmer months in addition to feeding upon frogs, toads and the spawn of both, plus newts and the eggs and young of moorhens and mallards (they also take the adult birds incidentally) when pickings are scarce in the winter, they maul or actually kill (though they never consume the entire carcass) specimen-sized carp weighing far heavier than themselves. Otters have in fact been responsible for killing carp to over 40lbs up and down the country.

16 When stalking for carp around really 'overgrown' lakes and pits or rivers, don't put pressure upon yourself by carting around the typical 'session-type' landing net comprising of a short pole and large, 42-45 inch arm, triangular net. Not only will it get easily tangled up whilst creeping about, beaten carp cannot always be hauled in close enough.

A strong, telescopic pole however, allows you to net fish that cannot be hauled close in through weed or lilies for a big net, and with a lightweight 24-30 inch round or spoon-shaped (deep-mesh) net on the end, you can capture fish of up to at least 40lbs when they lay beaten beyond the snags and marginal screen.

Above: Tip 17

Above Right:
Tip 18

17For targeting carp off the top when a fair amount of loose-fed floaters will get used during a lengthy session, invest in a 'bucket-organiser'. Mine has two strips of Velcro around the sides to which an organizer wallet is quickly fixed. This holds spare hooks, floating controllers, hair needles, mini hacksaw blades, super-glue and scissors etc, while the bucket itself contains several pints of mixers or floating pellets, plus catapult, and a few tubs of 'alternative' hook baits.

18When hair-rigging with particles, pellets or boilies, remember, (it takes but a few seconds) by using your thumb nail, to press the Dumbell-type, hard plastic hair stop completely into the bait so that it is hidden. With hard pellets, simply scrape out a depression with the end of your hair needle.

Carp (and barbel) have been purposefully-equipped with four ultra sensitive barbels which have minute sensory taste-pads on the end, in order to probe through gravel, sand and into deep silt to locate small, soft items of natural food. And if a carp can locate items such as midge larva, 'bloodworms' by feeling them with its barbel-tips, it is quite capable of reacting to hard, alien objects like a hair stop, and possibly refuse your bait as a result.

19There is a clear case for wearing shorts and a pair of old shoes or trainers when stalking summer carp amongst lilies and from amongst the branches of partly submerged trees. You can then quickly get in there to apply pressure from a different angle or to untangle a snagged fish, which you might otherwise lose, without second thought.

20To suit all your carping (tench and barbel) rig requirements during the summer ahead, tie up a selection of eyed hooks of varying sizes, each with varying length hairs to accommodate a variety of bait combinations.

Crucian Carp & Grass Carp

1 With massive introductions of king carp and carp hybrids to a large proportion of still water fisheries in the UK during the last 20 years, particularly 'commercial fisheries' as they are known, finding waters containing true crucian carp is now exceedingly difficult.

2 Most 'thought to be' record crucian carp submitted to the British Record Fish Committee, are in fact found, on close inspection, to be either crucian/ king carp crosses (paler, slimmer fish than true crucians with tiny barbels, sometimes referred to as F1 carp) or brown gold fish/ king carp/ or crucian crosses.

3 True crucian carp do not of course have barbels and rarely exceed 5lbs in weight. But they do have a slightly upturned mouth, are extremely deep-bodied, with rounded fins (which are an even, warm, grey-brown colour) and are distinctly 'buttery-bronze' in colour with flat-lying scales .If the fish you catch do not

Above: Tip 2

Left: Tip 3

Above: Tip 5

are immediately told apart by their low-set eyes, and dark grey anal fin. They characteristically 'hover' differently too, just beneath the surface on warm days with their head slightly upwards. And most importantly, in so far as the angler is concerned, they have a much smaller mouth.

6 Grass carp do not aggressively engulf their food like a chub. When seen sucking in small floaters from the surface they make a point of always 'pursing' the bait momentarily between their lips, before sucking it back a second later. So never be in too much of a hurry to strike. If through clear water you can observe your bait in the fish's lips, always wait until it totally disappears.

7 Here's a tip for fishery owners. Grass carp are the perfect fish for stocking into British waters, because they can not reproduce in our temperate climate. So what you stock (less predatory losses) is exactly what you end up with. They will therefore not hybridize with other carps or ever 'over-run' a fishery. Moreover, because they feed on vast quantities of soft plant tissue and do not compete directly with king carp, both can reach specimen sizes in the same fishery. What could be better?

conform to all these characteristics, then consider them not to be true crucian carp.

4 As crucian carp need to almost stand on their heads (just like a tench) to inhale a bottom fished bait such as sweet corn or bread flake, pinching on a small shot somewhere (it pays to experiment till bites become positive) between one and two inches from the hook, and to strike when the float tip 'lifts' momentarily. A scaled-down lift-float rig as used for tench (which are equipped with identical, slightly upturned mouths) using a smaller float, less shot and smaller hooks, is the way to catch the often 'shy-biting' crucian. Bites do not always take the float under.

5 Looking very much like a chub in the water (see Chub Tip 6) grass carp

8 Originating from lowland rivers in China such as the Amur, the fertilized eggs of grass carp need to float along the surface of running water at a temperature in excess of 65°F for many miles to stand any chance of hatching. Which is hardly likely in the UK.

9 Though fishing 'punched bread' is normally thought of as a winter technique for clear water canals, during the summer months it is deadly for the shy biting crucian carp. Use a 13 foot light, fine tipped stick float rod, dot the float tip right down, and using size 18-14 hooks, nick on small pieces of fresh white bread, removed from a medium slice with a bread punch head (most punches come with four or five different diameter screw-on heads)of the appropriate size. To complement punched bread on the hook, loose feed with 'liquidized bread' on the 'little and often' basis.

10 Vastly more effective than rod fishing, is to 'pole fish' using a light float rig to create a slow, natural fall of the bread during those last few inches above bottom. Shot the float right down to the merest 'blimp' so you can pull into the slightest sign of a bite.

11 Next to catfish and pike, grass carp are, pound for pound, the

Above: Tip 9

UK's longest freshwater species. How long will a 20lbs fish be? Possibly over three feet in length. Anything over 40lbs could measure four feet plus. Monsters of over five feet and weighing over 100lbs have been recorded in Europe, Africa and Asia.

12 Be most careful when handling grass carp out of the water. They are renowned for continually jumping and flapping about on the bank, often with more vigour than during the fight. So play each one till it is exhausted before heaving out and then cover securely with the wet mesh of your net till the hook has been removed.

13 When grass carp can be seen just beneath the surface or are suspected in the upper water layers but

are more appreciated without pole elastic to suppress and cushion their runs, and will give your forearm a good workout.

Use an ultra light float rig and shoot the bristle tip down to a mere 'whisker' in the surface film before accurately plummeting depth immediately below the tip of the Whip. Feed in maggots on the 'little' and 'often' basis (half a dozen around the float with every cast) after first introducing a few maggot-laced balls of cereal ground bait to concentrate a shoal of fish, and present a single maggot on a size 18 to 22 to a 1½lbs test hook length, exactly half an inch above the bottom.

15 Take a trophy photo of your big grass carp immediately after unhooking when it is at its most knackered. Hold it horizontally between your two hands, its head towards you not the water, 'upside down', yes 'upside down' (which immobilizes most fish incidentally) all ready for the photo and only turn it the right way up, once you are in position, a second before the shutter is released. Don't be tempted to let it recover in a sack or tube. Or you'll never be able to hold it still long enough for a photo.

16 Adding a single caster to your maggot hook bait, often makes

cannot be tempted to suck in a floater from the surface film, present a buoyant bait such as a pop-up boilie or floating pellet, bread crust even, (don't use anything larger than size 8-10 hooks) suspended between one and two feet below the surface. A scaled-down 'Zig-rig' (see Carp Tip 10) is perfect for this situation. Use a 'two rod' set up and try altering depths at which each bait is suspended, by recasting every half hour or so until a bite materializes.

14 Where the crucian carp of small, pea-green ponds and commercial fisheries average on the small side (say up to a pound in weight) it's great fun catching them in real close using just the top three or four joints of a lightweight pole or 'Whip', with a running line of say 2lbs test tied directly to the Whip's end ring. Their 'dogged' fighting capabilities

crucians 'hang-on' that much longer. Also worth trying is half a red worm.

17 At all costs do not try and catch crucian carp by ledgering. Due to their gentle feeding routine and sensitivity to resistance, you'll not even see most of the bites, let alone hit them, regardless of what indicator is used.

18 Crucian carp when feeding from the bottom, can be told apart from king carp varieties even when they cannot be seen simply by observing their 'feeding bubbles'. Those of even quite sizeable crucians for instance, rise gently to the surface in small clusters of just 4-6 bubbles tightly grouped together, which do not burst, compared with those of the king carp that are much larger, and which can be seen to burst after literally 'erupting' in the surface film.

19 As sweet corn is arguably one of the top hook baits for catching crucian carp, if you are uncertain about baits when tackling new crucian water, float fish corn with one large kernel on a size 14 hook, after adding the juices from the tin to some brown breadcrumbs to make a ground bait. Add a handful of 'squashed corn kernels' to the mix and feed on the 'little yet often' principle, keeping in mind that crucians are small carp.

20 Big, old specimen-sized crucian carp of say 2lbs and upwards can become extremely cagey if regularly fished for. The secret to catching them is to fish into darkness and well into the night, using the 'lift-method' (see Tip 4) with a 'luminous' chemical element sleeved onto a length of slim peacock quill attached bottom end only. Hold your rod throughout, ready to strike instantly as the float keels over flat. Some bites however will simply take the float under, sometimes quite fast, as the crucian characteristically 'runs' along the bottom with your bait. Bread flake, corn or worm are great 'after dark' offerings for big crucians.

Left: Tip 20

Catfish (Wels)

Below: Tip 1

1 For those wishing to land 100lbs-plus Wels catfish, the junction of where the River Segre joins the mighty River Ebro in the town of Mequinenza in North Eastern Spain is unrivalled. A two hour flight from Luton to Barcelona, followed by a two hour westerly drive from the airport to Mequinenza, gets you there. Contact The Bavarian Guiding Service whose offices and accommodation are adjacent to the river. Their website is: www.bavarian-guiding-service.de and for email enquiries: internationalfishingcamp@ntlworld.co.uk

2 For impromptu sessions after catfish (or pike, eels and carp etc - any fish where 'positive' runs are expected to the method being used) if the banks are nicely flat to the water, or if the swim is too difficult for bank

sticks, being fronted by stagings or a wall etc, then make your own 'bite alarm platform', simply by drilling and gluing the top two inches(hacksaw them off) from a couple of old bank sticks into a 12" x 4" x ¾" thick piece of ply or softwood. These are placed eight inches apart, into which a couple of bite alarms are screwed. Should you require 'rear' rests, then add rod rest tops (an inch or two higher) to another wooden platform. These take up far less room in your tackle bag than a collapsible 'rod-pod'.

3 Want to catch the hardest fighting freshwater species on this planet? Then the legendary Mekong catfish which has been netted to over 600lbs but is thought to reach weights in excess of 1000lbs is the adversary awaiting you in Thailand. Specimens up to 200lbs are purposefully stocked into many of Thailand's 'commercial' still-water fisheries, where they have been weaned onto and are readily catchable on simple baits like bread. The most prolific of Thailand's 'Mekong' fisheries is famous Bung Sam Ran near Bangkok. For guiding details contact: info@kiwifishingbangkok.com.

4 Whether fishing at home or abroad for tropical freshwater catfish, all catfish (including Wels catfish) quickly home in on the 'blood content' of baits whether freshly killed meat, fish or fowl. Chicken heads for instance, (yes beak and all, catfish don't worry about the bird's head when sucking down a duckling or moorhen from

Above: Tip 3

Above Left: Tip 2

killed eels, trout and small tench, with chunks of mackerel or squid topping the endless possibilities of sea baits. And of course when used together with a pre-baiting plan, of regularly loose feeding halibut pellets into British still water fisheries, the same large 20-30mm sized pellets presented anywhere from two to six up on a long hair rig, (use a 'daisy-chain' when offering 'several' pellets, to deter carp from getting hooked) have proved to be one of the most effective catfish baits of all.

6 To find out where you can fish for Wels catfish within the UK, contact the Catfish Conservation Group, who not only control cat fisheries for their members, they list all still waters in the UK that contain the species. Their website is: www.catfishconservationgroup.com.

7 Offal, readily available from your local butcher makes fine and exceptionally cheap bait for catfish. An ox heart for instance, which is getting on for the size of a rugby ball will separate down into between 8-12 blood-filled chunks, while a pig's heart makes two great offerings. And of course the kidneys and liver of

the surface) and their livers make fine baits. As do the heads of freshly killed pigeon, partridge and pheasant. All plucked of course. Simply present by hooking once only through the gristle using a size 3/0-6/0 hook (depending upon the size of catfish expected) and either ledger or free line.

5 If you have a buddy who shoots regularly, or you shoot yourself, a supply of plucked heads can be frozen away during the shooting season which ends in February, for use throughout the summer months. Other 'hot' catfish baits, for the Wels especially, are live and freshly

both animals are prime 'pussy-food'.
Though significantly smaller, sheep's
offal works well too.

8 Whilst there is little point in
trotting down live baits in British
river systems to catch catfish, because
stocking them into running water is
illegal, throughout Europe, particularly
certain Spanish rivers, The Ebro, The
Segre and The Sinca, trotting is a
'deadly' technique because it covers
so much water. Use a large 'through
the middle' catfish float stopped 3-5
feet above the hook trace with a bead
and power-gum stop knot. On the
two foot 150lbs test trace, joined to
an 80lbs braided reel line by a strong
swivel, with a barrel lead immediately
above, use a strong, size 6/0, wide-
gape hook. An ideal 'live-baiting'
pattern, and all-round cat fishing
hook is the Eagle Wave big game
whose unique shape in the middle of
the bend allows the bait maximum
movement and good penetration on
the strike. Top trotting baits are eels
and small carp.

9 Want to make your live bait even
more attractive? Well, how about
adding to your trace, two to three
inches above the hook, a designer

Left: Tip 8

'rattle'. These come in coloured plastic (white, red or yellow) and are fixed to the hook trace by laying the line in the hinge groove and snapping shut with ball bearing inside. A rubber float stop sleeved on either side, will prevent the rattle sliding. These incidentally have proved effective for pike, perch and for sea species.

10 To ensure your live bait stays on the hook, and this applies particularly to barb-less hooks, simply sleeve onto the hook after the bait, a designer 'Bait Shield'. Made from thick rubber, these unobtrusive discs, available from 'Catfish Pro' are also handy when using baits on a hair such as pre-drilled halibut pellets or soft baits like liver or squid, when normal boilie-type stops are simply too small.

11 By purchasing baby squid (calamari) in bulk, say several boxes at a time, from your local fishmonger or tackle specialist, there is no more economical way of ensuring throughout the summer months that you have enough suitable bait for both hook baits and loose feeding.

12 Presenting 5-8 inch live baits (rudd work well) just beneath the surface, especially during the hours of darkness, (using the 'Dumbell Rig') is one of the most effective ways of catching Wels catfish. As can be seen from the Diagram, after sleeving onto your reel line a 3-4 ounce lead

Below: Tip 12

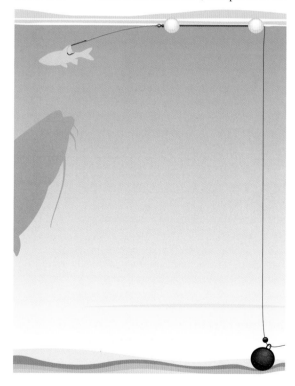

followed by a large rubber bead, the line is threaded through a 'Dumbell Float' and a small but strong swivel is tied on. Presentation is improved if the swivel pushes firmly into the end of the 'Dumbell Float', thus making it semi-fixed.

Lastly, add several inches of 'Catlink' braided trace material of 50-70lbs test and tie on a 2-3/0 hook, making sure the hook trace is slightly shorter than the length of the float, so that after casting and the lead touches bottom, when you tighten up to the float rig (lying flat on the surface) it is impossible for the bait to swim around the reel line and tangle. This is the beauty of this particular set up. Always use in conjunction with an electric bite alarm and indicator, as you may not always hear that glorious 'smack' of a cat engulfing your bait on the surface. This technique can be most effectively used with Tip 20.

13 For retaining catfish to photograph, use a long (6 foot x 18 inch diameter) 'Tunnel' or 'Tube' made from soft, black material, which opens at both ends with toggles for tethering to bank sticks and tension to keep straight.

Where really big fish are concerned, say 100lbs and larger, use a stringer made from soft, nylon cord.

14 For bringing big catfish into the boat when fishing abroad, especially in fast flowing rivers where landing nets are impracticable, wear a protective 'gripping' or 'chain mail' glove on each hand and with a firm two-handed grip of the fish's lower lip, haul it over the side, using the impetus of its own body movements to your advantage.

15 If you catch a Wels catfish which has just 'two' small barbels under its chin, instead of the normal 'four', you may not have caught a Wels, but an Aristotle's catfish (Silurus aristotelis) which originates from the Akheloos River in Greece, and which just might have found its way into British still waters (like so many alien species) through the ornamental pond-fish trade.

16 If you are limited in fishing hours or attempting to catch catfish from waters low in stock density, then 'prebaiting' can prove the answer to success. Introduce, say every other evening, generous helpings (especially if carp are present) of pelleted food

Centre: Tip 16

such as 'Halibut Pellets' (which break down and reduce to dust after 6-12 hours of being in the water) or 'Moggi Chunks' which come in both halibut pellet and fish-meal flavours, which break down somewhere between 24-48 hours.

17 Remember to set your rods 'well' back from the water's edge, and to be particularly quiet whilst fishing at night, as catfish love to hunt really close into the margins. So position one bait no more than a few yards out.

18 Watercraft plays an important part of targeting catfish during daylight hours. They love to lie up in the relative darkness and greatly reduced-light of beneath large, overhanging trees, sunken bushes and patches of lilies.

19 Fish care is so important when handling catfish. A giant unhooking matt is recommended as is a large, triangular landing net with 48-50 inch arms.

20 To present both live and dead baits at distances far greater than can be cast, (say 20 yards and beyond), try the unique 'Winching' method, which allows you to wind

or 'winch' (hence its name) your bait out to wherever you wish. Start by making up a simple end rig on your 15lbs test reel line, comprising of a 3-4 ounce bomb to which a link clip and ½ inch diameter curtain ring have been added, running above a snap-link swivel, with a large rubber bead in between. But don't attach your hook trace and bait just yet. And here's the clever part: have an extra rod (butt end only) ready, propped up with the butt ring facing the lake, the reel filled with just 4lbs test line, and the bale arm open, and tie the end securely to the snap link on your main outfit. Now cast out the heavy lead to where you intend fishing so that both lines go out over the lake.

Once your lead has settled place the catfish rod in two rests ready for action and open the reel's bale arm, so you can wind your snap link back using the half-rod, your 15lbs main line flowing freely through the curtain ring on the lead. Once the snap link has been retrieved, simply clip on your trace and bait and wind slowly back to the lead. And 'hey presto' your bait is now presented way out into the lake.

Chub

Far Right: Tip 6

1 Learn to walk slowly, when stalking chub, as though you are creeping up on rabbits in a field, picking up each foot individually (like a chicken does when it's stalking a worm) because I rate chub, particularly big, educated chub, by far the spookiest to bank side vibrations, of all our British freshwater species.

2 Never go chubbing without Polaroid glasses. I much prefer those with HLT, 'yellow' lenses (high light transmission lenses) which make viewing in dull, overcast conditions noticeably 'brighter'. Only in extra bright sunshine would I swap them for grey or amber lenses. A cap with a 'long' peak stops you moving your

hand up and down to shield your eyes from the sun. Less movement whilst 'fish spotting' results in more chub in the net.

3 Invest in a good quality, lightweight, pair of waterproof over trousers. You'll need them when kneeling, and crawling along 'Indian style', even during those early summer mornings, when marginal grasses are soaked with dew.

4 Learn to keep a sharp look-out for slugs during early morning trips, especially when it's drizzling. During the summer and autumn, there is no finer, more instant chub bait than a big brown or black slug, hooked once only through either end on a size 4

hook tied direct to a 6lbs reel line, and free-lined (no additional shots) alongside those difficult 'snag' swims. Watch the line from the second the slug hits the water. Most bites quickly tighten the line like a bowstring. Such is the ferocity of the take.

5 Never put your finger down a chub's throat to ease out a large eyed hook. Your forefinger will come out (after a loud yelp of pain) looking like it's been hit with a 3lbs hammer. Why? Because chub have large, powerful pharyngeal (throat) teeth, that's why.

6 How do you tell the difference between a chub and a grass carp? The chub's mouth is much larger, and the eye of the grass carp is set very low, in line with its jaw hinge. In addition, the grass carp's anal fin is grey whilst the chub's has an orange hue. Otherwise at a quick glance, especially in the water, they appear similar.

7 Enjoy weedy, seemingly impossible river conditions during the summer months with chub by catching them off the top on floating plugs. Good patterns are Big S style plugs, Meadow Mouse, and Big Bud etc. Weedless

CHUB

Below Tip 7

models are particularly effective. Use a short wire trace to alleviate being bitten off by the occasional pike.

8 By far the best winter feed for chub is mashed bread. Use stale scraps soaked in the sink and squeeze most of the water out before mashing between your fingers into a pulp. Its secret is that if old bread is used, it will sink quickly and break up into a million tiny fragments; thus attracting but not overfeeding.

9 Don't be surprised if you catch a big chub on small live baits intended for pike, perch or zander. They are one of our most voracious

freshwater predators. Try ledgering minnows or bleak, dead or alive, and how about half-inch chunks of eel or lamprey, which work well during the winter months. Loose feed sparingly with the same.

10 When long trotting for chub during the winter once the river bed has been scoured clean, use a wide-topped float (that can be easily see up to 30-40 yards) carrying a bulk shot of between 3-4 swan shot, but don't use swan shot. Instead bulk a line of AA shots 12-15 inches above the hook with a BB shot in between, so that just like a bath chain, the line of smaller shots 'bend' without pulling the float under, whenever the river bed shallows up. See Diagram.

11 Be careful using long nosed artery forceps when unhooking deeply hooked chub. It is so easy to crimp and severely weaken the line immediately above the hook. If in any doubt, simply tie the hook on again.

12 For a simple way of constructing a fixed paternoster ledger (which suffices for most of my 'static-bait' chub fishing incidentally) use the four turn water knot. Cut off 10 inches of reel line (or weaker if fishing amongst snags) and join to the main line 18-24 inches above the end. Tie the hook on last.

13 When chub in a clear flowing river are particularly finicky during the warmer months, procure a whole wasp (or hornet's) nest. Try the pest control department of your local council, or get your own, but be careful (shop bought preparations are available) and slowly bring

Left & Below:
Tip 10

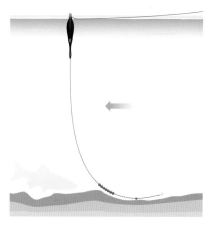

Above: Tip 15

Centre: Tip 16

chub upstream into a feeding frenzy close to the surface by loose feeding chunks of £2 coin-sized wasp nest (called 'cake') which includes grubs. When most of the shoal is up on the surface inhaling every piece you drift down, (it floats), put your hook in the next and free line on weightless tackle. You can virtually 'select' which fish you want. Wasp cake is truly 'magical' bait, and the large, succulent, white grubs can even be long-trotted one or two up on a size 12 hook whilst loose feeding with maggots.

14 Summer chub are absolute suckers on the fly rod for large 'imitative' nymphs presented upstream into the gravel runs they occupy between long flowing beds of weed. Get well below a shoal and offer a mayfly nymph on a long leader, remembering to recover line whilst watching it drift downstream. Strike at any unusual movement of the leader where it enters the water.

15 To bag up on chub using the bolt-rig style approach of a heavy running bomb, stopped 8-12 inches from the hook. Use a short ¾ -1 inch hair baited with a single 10-14mm pellet or boilie, or two size 10mm boilies or pellets, 3 grains of maize, etc, etc, while loose feeding with smaller attractor pellets, maize or sweet corn. For distance or really deep-water swims, pack loose feed plus the occasional hook bait sample into PVA tubing or bags and nick onto the bend of the hook, which will dissolve within minutes.

16 When ledgering across the flow in fast rivers, beware of those 'drop-back' bites where a chub moves towards you and thus makes the quiver tip spring back. In most cases it is not your bomb, feeder or link ledger shots

re-settling on the bottom. It is a chub. So strike instantly.

17 Don't bother using a separate weigh sling to weigh your specimen chub. If in the landing net it is already in a perfect receptacle. Simply unscrew the net top and hook it onto your scales, remembering to deduct its weight afterwards. What could be easier and less harm to the fish?

18 When downstream quiver-tipping or rod top ledgering, angle your rod pointing downriver with the flow at around 45 degrees to the bank, as opposed to out at right angles. You will then pick up much more line on the strike, and even connect with tiny indications that would otherwise be missed.

19 When chub become suspicious of floating crust, step down to smaller offerings like 'mixer biscuits' that you would use for carp. And simply present one super-glued onto a size 10 hook, (don't forget to cut a small groove in the biscuit with a junior hacksaw blade first) using a small controller float 3-4 foot above for casting distance, stopped by a small rubber cushioning bead and a 5 turn stop knot tied on with a few inches of reel line. See Carp Tip 4.

20 Concealment, stealth and camouflage are not just well worn words of hype from angling writers. They are the basic requirements to successful chubbing, particularly when exploring and slowly stalking clear and shallow, overgrown rivers and streams. So always creep about below the skyline, using the screen of tall grasses, shrubs and trees to full advantage. And above all, move slowly. It is that sudden 'movement' which instantly puts a wary chub on its guard.

Eel

1 With large eels in mind, one of the most successful baits, particularly in lakes or pits situated miles from the nearest river which contain only small numbers of adult eels, (often referred to as 'prison waters') is a couple of lobworms presented on a size 4 hook. It was in fact this very bait that produced the long-standing British record eel of 11lbs 2oz back in 1978 to the rod of Steve Terry.

2 As large eels are most sensitive to resistance, incorporate a large bore run ring into your running ledger rig, and use a lightweight indicator such as a simple coil of silver (kitchen) foil on the line between reel and butt ring, with an electric bite alarm as the front rod rest.

Strong runs should then develop from an open bale arm.

3 Hot, humid, pitch-black, thundery summer nights, provide the best opportunity of contacting sizeable eels, which at such times, often go on a feeding rampage.

4 In running water by far the best locations for targeting larger than average sized eels are weir and mill pools. But you'll need substantial tackle in pools where the bottom is full of junk, beneath which eels have their hideouts. This is 'hit, hold and wind' fishing at its most exciting.

5 During the autumn, vast numbers of eels 'silver-up' in readiness for their down river migration and journey to

procreate their species way across the Atlantic in the depths of the Sargasso Sea. Apart from a distinct change in colouration from yellowy, greeny-brown, to bright silver, their jaws noticeably broaden and become more powerful. They 'thicken–up' too.

6 Big eels can at times chew through even 10lbs test monofilament. So construct your hook traces from one of the new soft, multi-strand, Kevlar-twisted materials marketed especially for catfish enthusiasts. Alternatively, use a thin, multi-strand wire that is so supple it can be knotted.

7 Though not a 'sports-fishing' technique, 'Babbing' as it is commonly referred to, can provide a few hours fun during the hours of darkness, for anglers boat fishing during the summer months on eel-rich waters such as the Norfolk and Suffolk Broads.

8 To 'Babb' effectively, you need several dozen large lobworms, a ball of wool, ('Worstead' is best), and a long darning needle. Thread the worms onto the wool and wrap around your hand to form a 'wrap'. Secure the ends tightly around the wrap and tie onto 10-12 foot of strong cord (100lbs test braid is ideal) with a 2-3 ounce lead fixed a foot or so above the worms. Then tie to the end ring of an 11-12 foot (light to hold) shore rod.

9 When 'Babbing', the wrap of worms are lowered down to the river

bed, followed by the rod tip vibrating continually once eels are chewing on the worms. And, because their teeth 'catch' in the woollen yarn, they can be gently heaved out and lowered, all in one smooth, movement, straight into a large plastic bin. Don't worry about those which fall off. It's all part of 'Babbing'. You then have the choice of eating them immediately (simmering in milk in a saucepan produces a succulent meal of eel sections once they have been skinned) or freezing down for later use, either as sea baits for bass and tope, or for pike and zander.

10 If you happen to be friendly with a professional eel netsman (unfortunately they are a dying breed) there is no better or more informed person to point you in the direction of a 'big-eel water': a still water containing catch able numbers of specimen eels which for argument's sake, are in the 4lbs plus category. Purchasing a batch of smaller eels from him to freeze down as winter pike baits, might loosen his tongue.

11 Whilst eel fishing is invariably much better at night when they come out to play, the eels inhabiting deep reservoirs and gravel pits are likely

to hunt, and consequently feed, at any time of the day, particularly during low light conditions.

12 Use a powerful, but 'all through action' rod when targeting eels. One that will bend in harmony with a 10-15lbs test monofilament reel line, and so not cause the hook to rip out, or induce the trace to fracture when the eel comes close in under the rod tip, and is on a short line ready for netting.

13 'Prison waters' invariably contain the largest freshwater eels of all. Lakes or ponds, modest-sized irrigation reservoirs or pits (even the tiniest of farm ponds) that are miles from the nearest river or brook. Such waters may not have been reached by many eels during their upstream migration, but those which made it, are likely to grow to a very large size, due to minimal competition for food.

14 Many 'prison' waters, especially small pits and farm ponds etc, give their best results during your initial few trips simply because they contain so few (albeit large) eels. So if results dwindle rapidly after say two or three trips, accept the fact that you may well have either caught, pricked, lost or simply scared virtually the water's entire

Left: Tip 14

Far Left: Tip 12

eel population. So move on.

15 To weigh your specimen eel (and anything from 4lbs upwards is a 'target fish'), simply unscrew the landing net top and hoist onto the scales after removing the hook. Grip the eel firmly behind its head on the outside of the net, using the mesh as a gripping agent when extracting the hook. Then deduct the net's weight afterwards. It's so much easier and much less slime is transferred from eel to you, than by attempting to transfer it into a separate weigh sling.

16 To take a trophy shot of a specimen eel do so immediately after capture and unhooking when it is at its most knackered. If you leave in a sack or tube till dawn, by which time it will have recovered, taking any kind of decent photo will prove almost impossible.

17 In really large still waters where feature, hideout-habitats such as bridges, old boat houses, islands, dam walls, sunken boats or cars, etc, are evident or known to you (in the case of sunken boats or cars) be prepared to move about and change swims regularly following every measure of success, because many of the very largest eels will occupy those

'choice' habitat hideouts.

18 Do not be tempted into using large hook baits simply because you are seeking large eels. Big baits can cause more trouble than they are worth when it comes to deciding 'when' to strike a positive run. Small, slim-bodied, freshly killed fish, (and 'freshly killed' is most important here) such as gudgeon, bleak, dace, roach or rudd of between three and four inches in length are ideal. Odd ball baits like the entire insides of a large swan mussel, or a baby 'calamari' (squid) are also worth trying.

19 To mount a small fish bait for optimum hook-ups, use a size 6-2 wide gape, strong hook, and push once only through the tail root. Work the hook along the baits flank (just beneath the skin) so it comes to lie immediately behind the gills with the point and

bend of the hook nicely exposed. See Diagram. Just like pike, eels usually turn their prey to swallow head first so the fish's fins go down the gullet easily, and so a hook positioned immediately behind the gills usually finds purchase, despite the tail protruding from the eel's mouth. If you use a multi-hook rig, then use a wire trace in case a pike gobbles up your dead bait.

20 When striking, close the reel's bale arm gently (vibrations might travel down the line) and point the rod directly at the eel, waiting for the line to pull tight. Then, in one smooth, easy action, haul the rod back into a full curve and start winding. Big eels immediately pull back using that inherent 'snake-like' motion of their bodies, or actually run off. So make sure the clutch on your reel will yield line under pressure.

Below: Tip 19

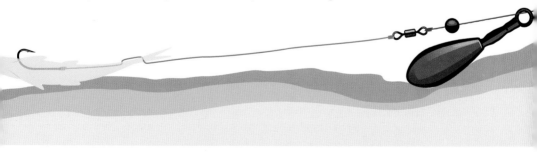

Grayling

1 When long-trotting for her ladyship the grayling, do not be tempted to fish with too light a shotting pattern, or dot the float tip down as though 'stick-float' fishing. Grayling are the boldest biters of all, even in the coldest weather. Wide-topped 'chubber-style' floats, that can easily be seen 30-50 yards downstream (yes you can hit bites at such distances in fast water) carrying between two and five swan shot are perfect for the job, but don't use swan shots. A line of AA sized bulk shot pinched on 12 inches above a size 14, forged hook with a No 1 or BB shot half way between is far better, because like a bathroom chain, it 'bends' when passing over stones and silt without

pulling the float under, allowing the bait to drag bottom beautifully. See Diagram for Chub Tip 10.

2 Even in clear, really cold water, grayling will still pull the float down boldly so long as the bait is presented just above bottom, and within their line of sight. You can easily distinguish between male and female grayling by the different shapes of their dorsal fins. Males have a long 'sail-like' dorsal which when opened out almost touches their adipose fin, while females have smaller, almost 'square-shaped' dorsals when opened out.

3 The only conditions when grayling won't play ball and bite confidently in cold weather is when the river is

swollen over the banks full of dirty, milky-tea floodwater. They then seem loathe to move towards a trotted bait, perhaps on account that it cannot be seen clearly anyway. Switching over to stret-pegging tactics with a couple or three maggots, or a small red worm anchored hard on the river bed, and introducing loose feed directly down to the bottom by way of a 'bait-dropper', will sometimes produce, as will quiver-tip ledgering in conjunction with a small block-end feeder rig.

4 After grayling, trout, pike, chub and dace (in that order) are the most likely species to bite in a freezing

river. Remember that in sub-zero temperatures their metabolism will have slowed down to a snail's pace, and with chub and dace only tiny bite registrations are expected even to small 'static' baits on tiny hooks, which is why trotting enthusiasts love grayling so much.

5 If you cannot get to a tackle shop in time for some maggots or fail to find red worms in the compost heap, and you have a day's trotting for grayling already booked, then worry not. Grayling are real suckers for sweet corn, trotted down just like maggots. Some think that sweet corn's resemblance in size to the eggs of salmon, upon which grayling gorge at times (which is why the species is so unwelcome on prize salmon beats and treated with disgust) is what makes grayling accept it so readily. So it's always worth keeping a tin or two in the boot of the car, particularly coloured sweet corn, which in 'orange' looks uncannily like salmon eggs. Red works effectively too.

6 Long trotting for grayling in clear-flowing southern chalk streams is not, as many seem to think, only for the privileged or the rich. The fishery managers and keepers of many highly-

prized trout fisheries along rivers such as the Test and the Kennet, where grayling abound, actually encourage responsible anglers to enjoy this winter pursuit between the months of November and March. Simply enquire at tackle shops in towns like Stockbridge and Andover in Hampshire and in Newbury and Hungerford in Berkshire.

7 As with big dace, there is very often a segregation of the sexes with grayling towards the end of the coarse fishing river season, in preparation towards their eventual spawning during April, with the big males, being either loners or grouped in twos or threes, and now noticeably darker in colouration, dominating many of the choice lies.

Above: Tip 6

Far Left: Tip 4

8 Summer or winter, grayling are always great fun to catch on the fly rod. With smaller, more intimate rivers in mind where short casting will cover most runs, a two ounce, wand-like carbon brook rod coupled to a lightweight reel and size 4 weight-forward floating line, allows the grayling to really show you what it can do. Use just a 2½ -3lbs test tippet and plan to plop your artificial in at the head of each run (exactly where you would start trotting a float) from a position directly downstream. So plan to wade swims that demand it.

9 When fly fishing upstream for grayling, weighted patterns like the

leaded shrimp and tin head or gold head nymphs on size 10 hooks are favourite, and you need to be continually retrieving the loose line as the nymph comes back downstream towards you with the current, your eyes 'glued' to where the leader enters the surface, because sometimes, you'll get little more than a quick 'forward twitch' to pull into.

10 Many fly fishermen attach a buoyant, highly visible 'sight-bob' to the leader 2-6 feet above the fly (depending on depth of the run being covered) which in effect acts just like a float and registers a bite instantly a grayling inhales the artificial.

11 Whether long trotting or presenting the upstream nymph to grayling during the winter months, so you can sit comfortably low down on the bank side, kneel when required, or easily wade into a prime casting position, even wade fully across the river in order to cover choice swims along the opposite bank, its worth investing in a pair of good quality, lightweight, breathable chest waders which have neoprene feet as opposed to rubber boots. Brogue-type leather or canvas wading boots with felt soles are

then worn over the neoprene, sock feet, providing excellent support for either wading over slippery stones in fast currents, or wandering along the banks.

12 The wandering, exploring grayling angler carries neither holdall nor tackle bag. All tackle sundries such as fly boxes, floats, silicon float bands, hooks, shots, disgorger and forceps etc, are carried on his person in a waistcoat. A waistcoat with a tab and D ring on the back to accept the clip of a collapsible flick-up type landing net suits both the fly fisherman and long-trotter alike. There are times, however, when predominantly bank fishing over wide beds of reed and sedge, that a separate long handled landing net is required by the long trotting enthusiast.

13 An indispensable item of tackle when long trotting for her ladyship the grayling, is a simple two division 'bait pouch'. One for maggots and the other to hold red worms or sweet corn. This belts around the waist and alleviates the necessity of continually having to open bait boxes with freezing cold finger tips, to say nothing of carrying said boxes. When tackling wide rivers, a catapult is

handy too.

14 Southern chalk streams have hatches of flies just about every day of the calendar year, and you can differentiate between a trout and a grayling sucking down an emerging or floating adult insect by the type of splash it creates. Look for the perfectly 'round' ring of the grayling feeding off the surface.

15 Small dry flies, anything in the 'olive' range are readily taken as are sedges and mayflies. A grey wulff is one of the better 'larger' patterns when it comes to sizeable grayling.

16 A small lightweight plastic bait dropper is very handy for ensuring that loose feed goes directly down along the bottom of deep and extremely turbulent gravel runs, which would otherwise send hand-fed maggots off in all directions and at all levels, scattering the shoal in the process.

17 The nice thing about grayling is that once the float has been set at the correct trotting depth to present the bait trundling along just above the river bed, there is little point in making any more than three or four trots through before moving on to the next run. Because if grayling are present, a bite

will usually come at the first or second run through.

18 When tackling the grayling of shallow and clear flowing chalk streams where everything can be clearly seen, a positive plan of action which always works for me, is to first walk the entire fishery upon arrival starting from the downstream boundary up, making note of those swims which contain the most or the largest fish and where big trout or the odd salmon are lying, in order to avoid them. All the way upstream to the top boundary. Then walk and fish the entire fishery downstream along which everything will by now have settled.

19 Top chalk stream features much loved by larger grayling, are tiny, but deep hatch pools, deep runs close into the bank, even those of just a few yards in length, and those long, even paced, even-depthed glides with a clean sandy bottom.

20 Be prepared during an exhaustive day's long trotting to change your hook several times. The tell-tale sign of your hook becoming blunt is when a maggot becomes difficult to impale or bursts as you nick it on.

Perch

1 Of all top techniques for catching perch during the winter months, once the weed in lakes and rivers has died back, particularly those wily old 'big perch', 'back-ledgering', is the most deadly, because through 'minimal casting' it creates less disturbance. Go for a two rod-approach, employing a simple 'fixed paternoster' ledger rig on each, with a couple of 2x or 3x swan shots (depending upon casting distance or current strength) on the 10 inch weight link, and a large, gyrating lobworm nicked onto a size 4, on the 20 inch hook length.

2 For 'back-ledgering in rivers (quiver-tip rods are actually recommended here because the fine, forgiving tips are less likely to pull the hook from a

lightly hooked perch) cast one rod as far downstream as you can, and the second around half the distance. And catapult in several helpings of broken lobworms down the entire length of the swim between the far bait and the end of your 'near' rod, to get the perch in a feeding mood. And continue introducing broken worms throughout the session when fish

Above: Tip 5

are coming regularly.

3 When back-ledgering, both rods should be 'almost 'pointing at the baits. I say almost, because if set in the rests at a slight angle, gentle pulls and the start of a bite is often shown on the quiver tip before the bobbin actually moves. And so striking can be pre-empted. Then clip on a lightweight bobbin-type

indicator between reel and butt ring. An electric bite alarm used as a front rod rest incidentally, comes in very useful when sport is slow, and you don't want to miss out by day dreaming.

4 The secret of 'back-ledgering, is every 10-20 minutes or so, to remove the bobbin and gently lift up each rod whilst winding the reel's handle between

one and a couple of turns, thus moving the worm off the bottom (it will 'flutter' down beautifully) towards you. Then put the rod down, wind up slightly and clip on the bobbin. A drop of around 12-14 inches is ideal. But sometimes you will barely have time for this because a perch will have nailed your lobworm 'on the drop'. Remember to keep those 'broken' worms going in throughout the session, or bites may dry up.

5 Where do big perch live? Well, due to 'summer weeds' dying back, when fry shoals tend to mass together for protection in deeper holes and gullies, larger perch then subsequently tend to group-up in catchable numbers close by. So in still waters such as lakes and gravel pit complexes, if you are not aware of the water's bottom topography, spend some time plumbing the depths to locate those choice, deeper areas. Marginal features such as an old boat house built adjacent to deep water, beneath overhanging and part-sunken trees and dam outlets, are also worth exploration.

6 In river systems, with the biggest perch in mind, look for 'top-habitat swims', where large bushes and trees overhang the water, especially where willows dunk their lower limbs below

Far Left: Tip 6

the surface, and keep an eye out for those big perch-swims par excellence: beds of dense bull rushes. Both habitats harbour perch because they provide great ambush points. The dark, vertical stripes of the perch blend in perfectly with the stems of the bulrush and with the subsurface stems of the willow. Around lock gates, beneath road bridges and beside pilings are also favoured, as are the 'holes' on acute bends and 'cut-backs' along thick beds of sedges hugging the margins. Also, see Tips 12 and 13.

7 Serious big-perch specialists are very selective about when they fish, and keep a keen track of winter weather patterns. Because while perch are possibly likely to feed at any time regardless of temperatures, by far the 'hottest' feeding periods, in rivers especially, occur during spells of extra-mild weather. Wait till temperatures do not fall below zero for several consecutive nights, rising to maybe 10 or 12 degrees during the day, and get out there pronto, making the most of conditions till the next cold snap.

8 When ledgering small live-baits for perch (gudgeon, dace, roach and little perch are best – in that order) I favour a reel line of around 6lbs test matched to an Avon-style ledger rod of 11-12 feet.

On the business end is tied a wide-gape size 4 eyed hook, to 20 inches of reel line and a small swivel. Above this goes a 'cushioning' rubber bead and a running snap swivel with 4 inch heavy mono 'link' and one ounce bomb attached. Any lighter and the bait might 'tow' the lead around.

9 Always angle the rod tip downwards supported on two rests and pointing directly at the bait to minimize resistance, when ledgering small live baits for perch. For bite indications hang a simple 'bobbin' on a 20 inch drop between reel and butt ring, pinching a swan shot or two on the retaining cord to counteract excessive movement from the bait.

10 To ensure the single hook is not impaired on the strike when live baiting, hook the bait fish once only through its chin membrane or both nostrils, and slip on over the barb, a ¼ inch square of 'rubber band'. This alleviates the bait flying off during the cast or at any other time.

11 That old saying 'that the best bait to catch a big perch, is a little perch', is on most occasions, perfectly true. Next to gudgeon which seem to possess 'magical' powers of attraction to 'big stripies', a small live perch of

Right: Tip 12

Far Right: Tip 13

around 4–5 inches long is indeed hard to beat because large perch become so, by consuming large quantities of their own brethren in addition to other small silver-shoal species.

12 Just like barbel, river perch adore bulrushes. Not those tall dark brown, cigar-like seed heads of the greater reed mace, often wrongly referred to as bulrushes, but the cylindrical, dark-green onion-like stems which protrude through the surface from a gravel bed and which can be seen 'quivering' often in huge marginal clumps as well as through the middle of a shallow river, as the strong current bows them slightly over. A few inches below their pointed tops are fragile, light-brown seed heads, so very different from reed mace.

13 It is most important to differentiate between the two plants above because they each prefer different habitats. Perch love true bulrushes because their vertical stripes blend in remarkably well with the erect stems, affording them marvellous ambush opportunities, from where they can attack small silver shoal species, using minimum effort.

But if you cannot obtain small live baits don't worry. A juicy lobworm or dendrobena trotted along just above bottom beneath an 'Avon-style' or 'chubber' float produces the most gloriously positive bites. Free lining a big worm into gaps between the bulrushes, and allowing it to free-fall to the bottom as it drifts along will also produce aggressive 'chub-like' bites; the line 'zinging' tight after a preliminary twitch or two.

14 One of the best, or 'worst'-kept secrets about commercial carp-type fisheries, where the perch, if stocked often get neglected, is the size they grow to. Specimens over 3lbs being common place, due no doubt to the amount of loose feed in the way of casters, maggots and worms that are used to attract carp and silver shoal species. If you add the fry of silver shoal species that breed in these albeit small, but prolific waters, you don't have to be a rocket scientist to realize that 'commercial water' perch, are extremely well fed. Reason enough to be the odd man out by specifically targeting them.

15 A simple running paternoster ledger rig presented beneath a small (through the middle) sliding float is the best way of live baiting for big perch, because it keeps your bait continually working over the targeted area. Whereas free-roaming live baits

all too easily dive into weed or beneath trees or vacate the area all together when predators show up.

16 To rig a sliding float (using a tiny bead and five turn stop knot above) set it a little deeper than the swim, with the 6lbs test main line threaded through one end of a swivel and tied to the hook link swivel (with a small bead between) and a wide gape size 4 on the business end of the 16 inch hook length. To the loose swivel above the bead (which now becomes the 'bomb link) tie 20-30 inches of 8lbs mono and add a one ounce bomb.

Small roach, rudd, gudgeon and dace etc, are ideal baits and work continually if simply hooked through both nostrils. Remember to angle the rod top high in order to keep as much line out of the water as possible.

17 To stand a chance with the largest perch of all, concentrate on the species during the last few weeks of the river fishing season leading up to the middle of March, when due to increased temperatures they will be looking to feed heavily prior to their eventual spawning during April.

18 Don't be tempted to hedge your bets whilst offering live baits to perch and incorporate a wire trace in case a pike happens along. Perch, the whoppers especially, are particularly sensitive to a wire trace. Besides, should a pike bite through your 6lbs reel line, it will either quickly get rid of a large single, bronze hook, or the hook will rot and rust away within weeks.

19 During the warm summer months, below the churning, well oxygenated white water of a weir pool, immediately below the sill, and in the corresponding eddies on both sides, are areas much favoured by big, river perch. Vast shoals of newly hatched fry gather in such places and perch are only too aware of the fact. Try a small diving plug or float-fished live bait like a bleak or a gudgeon set around mid-depth. Your float won't be on the surface for too long.

20 Beware of striking float-fished live baits too hard. Simply tighten down once the float has disappeared and wind up tight till you can 'feel' the fish, before pulling the rod tip back and winding in one smooth movement, continuing to wind so the hook finds purchase as the perch tries to eject the bait by shaking its head violently from side to side.

Far Left: Tip 17

Pike

1 To handle pike safely and carefully for both a trophy photo and during the process of unhooking, use a chain mail glove on your left hand (the Rapala 'Fillet Glove' is perfect for the job and will fit either hand) and gently slip four fingers into the pike's left gill opening, being very careful not to touch its gill rakers. When your fingers are fully in, press down tightly on the outside (against your forefinger) with your thumb. Don't relax your grip or the fish might escape.

To remove hooks with long nosed-artery forceps, (imperative) simply curl your left hand slowly, and 'hey presto' the pike's lower jaw will open. It has no option because being part of its bony skull the top jaw has little movement anyway.

It really is so easy, and small fish can even be unhooked with most of their body still in the water, or when held vertically. For maximum support, big fish are best laid on their back on an unhooking mat during the unhooking process. Hooks deep down are most easily removed by going in with the forceps through the opposite gill opening.

2 When float fishing at distance in still water use 'hi-viz' sliding pike floats that incorporate dart-type, 'sight-vanes', and remember to use 3-4mm rubber 'cushioning beads' either side of the float, between float eye and trace swivel. And between float eye and a sliding stop knot, tied onto the reel line above the float at the required depth, using a few inches of 10-15lbs test, red (easy to see) power gum.

Left: Tip 3

separate weigh sling is really not required.

Now is the time for a photo, following unhooking, immediately prior to release when they are at their quietest.

Endeavour therefore, not to retain a large pike in a keep-sack or tube for any length of time in order to capture a picture of it. Unless of course torrential rain precludes this at the time of capture. Truth is, once pike have regained their strength by resting in a sack, they become unbelievably difficult to hold still. And at best you will become heavily covered in their protective slime as they wriggle about. So for the sake of both pike and angler, immediate release is always recommended.

Don't trim the ends too short (leave both 1½ inches long) or the knot will catch against the rod rings during casting, and inhibit distance.

3 To weigh 'trophy-sized' pike, it's far easier (especially on the pike) immediately after landing when they are still in the folds of a large (already wet) net. One with arms around 40-42 inches in length will accommodate the biggest specimens, and you simply detach the arms from the spreader block and roll the net up before hooking the scales on halfway along, remembering to deduct the weight of the net afterwards. What could be easier? After which, the pike is laid onto a foam-filled unhooking mat, either still in or out of the landing net, and the hooks are removed. A

4 Some anglers tend to think that because the pike is a marauding killer with an enviable array of backward-pointing teeth covering the roof of its upper jaw, in addition to the long, powerful canines set into the lower jaw and thus capable of engulfing, drowning and swallowing water birds as large as mallards, that it should be shown perhaps less stealth, than say the chub. But they would be wrong. So acute are the senses of pike, even totally 'blind' fish are confident at lunging into a shoal of bait fish or striking at an artificial lure. Smelling out static dead baits resting on the bottom is by comparison, child's play of

don't have to catch live baits first, and while a pike is likely to turn up anywhere except the main flush, I favour any slow back eddy close into the bank. Especially those lies beneath overhanging trees. Guaranteed hot spots these.

Small areas of slack water beneath redundant hatch gates are also worth attention, as are any areas of slow, deep water. So, study surface currents seriously for several minutes before making that initial cast. Sometimes slacks occur in the pools centre, and to keep live bait out there use a float-paternoster rig incorporating a 'heavy' bomb, and angle the rod tip high to keep most of the line off the surface between float and tip.

course. This predator has in fact survived in British rivers and lakes for at least half a million years. Fossil remains found in Germany, date back to 20 million years ago.

5 Mill and weir pools are great meeting places for all river species. And because the occupants must keep moving in the fast currents, thus consuming more energy than still-water fish, they need to feed more regularly, even throughout the coldest winter conditions; pike included. In water running low and clear, best results usually come to trotted live baits just above bottom, or working lures. A big spoon is my favourite, which with just the one treble hook at the rear, catches up on fewer snags than say, diving plugs.

Wobbling dead baits is another extremely effective 'weir pool' technique which maximizes on time because you

6 For free lining dead baits to pike in both still and running water, even, and especially when boat fishing, the most effective bite indicator (used with the reels bale arm open) is a loop of line retained beneath an elastic band on the rod handle immediately opposite the reels spool. This is 'sensitivity' personified because you can make the band as forgiving or as tight as conditions dictate (to combat fast river currents or a strong sub-surface 'draw' in still water for instance) and once the loop has pulled out, line simply peels from the spool without the slightest resistance.

Always pinch a couple of swan shots onto the wire trace just below the swivel to initiate the pike moving directly away and giving a 'positive' bite indication.

7 If fishing 'tidal rivers' for pike, remember the most likely time for a spot of action particularly when sport is slow due to freezing conditions etc, is when the tide changes. Either from flooding to the ebb or visa versa, when all species including pike must change position in order to once again face the flow. And that period when fish are moving about just before the change, to when the river has swapped direction and is flowing in the opposite direction is not only critical, on a bad day it is very often the only occasion pike will find your baits.

8 If you are fed up with sitting frozen to the bone waiting for one of the baits presented on a multiple-rod set up to be taken, then here's a tip, based on my preference to be continually moving, called my 'spoon and static' approach. A highly mobile technique I employ when searching previously un-fished rivers and lakes for pike, guaranteed to keep you warm.

I use two 9 foot rod outfits, one of which sports a fixed spool reel (could be a multiplier) loaded with 12lbs mono, plus wire trace and a 5 inch spoon. The second reel is a 6501-sized (left-hand wind) multiplier loaded with 30lbs test braid and wire trace holding a duo of size 8 semi barb-less trebles. I start by selecting a likely area, pinch on two 2x swan shots onto the wire trace immediately below the swivel, fix on dead bait such as a smelt, mackerel tail, or whole sardine, and cast it out. Once the bait has touched bottom I lay the rod on the ground pointing at the bait, without worrying about rod rests and bite indicators and wind the loose line reasonably tight. The reel is then clicked into free spool and the ratchet engaged. This is my audible bite indicator. I then search the surrounding territory with the spoon-outfit, retrieving it close to the bottom in an erratic, fluttering, wounded-fish action, with the rod tip pointing directly at the lure to maximize on the hooks going home when a pike lunges at it.

I'll spend no more than say 15-20 minutes in any spot, before 'twitching' the static back (in case it gets grabbed on the move) and then move on to the next likely swim. There are days when pike really want a chase and the fluttering spoon scores, and times when only the static is taken, usually quite quickly too, within 5-10 minutes of being cast. And of course there are days when both methods produce.

9 Now here is a really top, top tip. That old adage of offering a 'big' bait if you are after a big pike, does not necessarily add up. What does happen in many cases is that with larger baits, the problems of hooking-up are far greater. Personally, whether live or dead baiting, I much prefer whole fish or half baits in the 5-7 inch size bracket. I can then point the rod at the pike and wind down till the line is completely 'tight', before striking immediately, all in one progressive action, knowing that I have more than a fair chance of the hooks finding purchase.

10 For ledgering static dead baits in deep, fast, coloured rivers, use aromatic species such as the 'cucumber' smelling smelt and grayling, or blood-saturated fish like lampreys and eels, especially the head-ends that have huge blood content. Mackerel and herring heads also work very well.

Initial 'knocks' on the rod tip (which should be angled up high to ensure maximum line is out of the water) signal a pike mouthing the bait, after which line will evaporate quickly from the reel. So either use a multiplier in free spool with the ratchet on, a loop of line set tightly beneath an elastic band on the rod handle with the reel's bale arm open, or a 'bait-runner' reel.

Alternatively, the rod tip might suddenly 'spring back' denoting a pike has dislodged the ledger weight whilst taking the bait, but if line fails to pull from the reel, it's because the pike has swum towards the rod. So wind down instantly, and 'feel' for that tell-tale 'knocking' of a fish already on.

11 When targeting the big pike of my local Norfolk Broads during the coldest, most featureless time of the year between December and March when the marginal cover of reeds and sedges has died back and their baitfish prey lack cover, a large percentage of the fish I'm after will be well out from the bank on the bottom of the 'bowl' (many of the shallower broads are like a saucer in cross-section) in the deepest section. And for this kind of pike fishing, I find that systematically 'grid-

Right: Tip 11

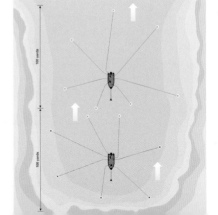

searching' the middle reaches of the broad, pays best dividends.

After putting the mud weights down at the most 'upwind' area (with a view to subsequently simply lifting them and allowing the wind to take me down to the next position) rods are fanned all around the boat presenting static dead baits, using a mixture of float-fished and free-lined smelt and lamprey heads, with the tip of each rod pointing directly at the bait. The idea being to cover every angle of where a pike might be lying or approach the bait from. Then if nothing materializes within say an hour after repositioning each bait a couple or three times, then the mud weights are silently lifted to try the next area downwind. This technique certainly produces a high proportion of quality-sized double figure fish, (not to mention the occasional whopper) which show a distinct preference for static dead baits. See Diagram.

12 Fancy making your 'own' traces up for pike. It is not only cheaper than purchasing tackle shop 'pre-mades', you have total choice in what patterns of hooks and swivels are used, plus the type of wire they are presented on. And if the trace lets you down, you only have yourself to blame. But because making your own is so much cheaper, you will automatically replace each one immediately it becomes doubtful through 'fraying' or bent hooks, etc.

Essential items include a selection of trebles and swivels (may I suggest size 10 swivels and size 8 semi barb-less trebles will suffice for most pike fishing) a roll of 30lbs test 'easy-twist' braided wire, and a small pair of quality wire cutters. A 'twiddle stick' which has a 'shepherd's crook' at one end for twisting the tab end of the wire around itself, to secure treble or swivel, (though this can be done with your bare fingers) not only makes constructing traces so much easier, but more professional-looking. See Diagram.

Start by cutting off around 24 inches of wire and (assuming you are right-handed) holding a treble in your left hand, with your right, pass one end of the wire through the eye, and then a second time to form a loop. Now pass the end through the loop to form a simple 'clinch' and gently pull evenly on both strands of wire to reduce the loop into a tight knot. Using your left hand catch the crook of the twiddle stick around one prong of the treble and slowly revolve towards you, whilst with your right hand (holding the tab end of wire between thumb and forefinger) carefully guide it around itself in neat coils. After a dozen or

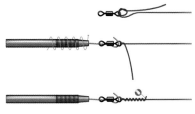

so coils, snip off the end.

Slide on the second treble (through the eye) and secure two to three inches above the first treble by gently wrapping the wire three or four times around the shank. To complete the trace, repeat the 'twisting' procedure by adding a swivel to the other end. And there it is. Job done. Traces end up around 20 inches long (after twisting and trimming) so that should the bottom few inches of wire become 'kinked' or 'frayed' after catching a pike or two, cutting off the suspect length of wire and replacing the trebles takes but a jiffy. And your trace is still long enough for action, though a few inches shorter. Make up 'spinning traces', (12-14 inches long) with a plain swivel at one end and a snap swivel at the other, in exactly the same way.

13 Here's a tip for catching cold-water pike in ultra low temperatures when they lie on the bottom (covered in double-sucker leeches on their fins and gill plates) and show not the slightest interest in food unless it passes within mere inches of where they lay motionless. To ensure your lure or wobbled dead bait works only within this critical, cold-water depth band, less than two feet above bottom, try adding a 12 inch 'stiff' mono link and running swivel immediately above the trace swivel (with a small bead between) with a half ounce bomb on the end. You can then twitch and wobble your dead bait or lure in ever so slowly, only tightening up when you feel a take.

14 When trotting down live or dead baits for river pike, use an in-line, sliding, 'Tenpin-style' buoyant float through which the reel line passes and is stopped at the desired depth by a small bead and five turn stop knot, tied with power gum. Bulk shot in the way of two to three large swan shots or a large oval bullet (cushioned by a rubber bead) should sit on the main line immediately above the trace swivel.

The beauty of using the 'sliding Tenpin' is that at any point along the swim where the bottom is known to shallow up or there is a snag, you simply ease the stop knot a few feet above the float by holding the rod tip high, and then let it go again when depth resumes. In addition, this is the perfect rig for 'stret-pegging' dead baits static on the bottom of fast flowing rivers.

15 To rig the sliding 'tenpin' or any other 'through the middle' pike float for 'stret-pegging', simply exchange the shots or oval bullet for a running 1-2 ounce bomb, and slide the stop knot up to several feet deeper than the swim. Then cast directly downstream, and allow a 'subsurface bow' to form in the line between float and terminal rig, so that the float actually lies 'flat' on the surface. The 'flat float' creating minimal resistance to a pike sucking up the bait.

16 Want the most durable of all baits to use for a day's 'wobbling' for pike where continual and long casting are prerequisites? Well, look no further than 5 to 7 inch rainbow trout which have unbelievably firm bodies and last for ages. You can purchase them frozen from specialist tackle shops, or, and you may well be obliged to buy these in bulk, enquire at your local trout farm or fishery where small disfigured and freshly dead trout are removed daily from the stews. When mounted on a duo of size 8 semi barb-less trebles (the top in an eye socket and the lower down the flank) with a slight 'bend' set in the trout's body a lovely action is produced.

17 For 'popping-up' light, smallish whole dead baits such as roach, smelts or sprats, etc above bottom silt and weed, simply twist a 2-3 inch link of soft multi-strand wire onto to the shank of the lower treble on your standard two-hook wire trace. Then, at the other end, twist-on a 'green' ¾ inch diameter 'Pro Popper' soft foam buoyant ball to raise the bait's head and torso off the bottom. Pinch a 2 or 3x SSG shot onto the wire trace a few inches from the bait's tail, (to ensure it rises the exact distance required above bottom) and another next to the trace swivel. It works an absolute treat, and pike are not put off, because the foam ball is 'soft'. For popping up larger baits simply use two small foam balls, instead of one larger one, which could impair striking.

18 When after the huge pike of trout reservoirs, there are two kinds of fish-holding features to look for: visual features such as valve towers, the dam wall and around the cages where trout are fed daily in the floating stews, and unseen features, which only become apparent when using an echo-sounder/fish-finder unit. These might consist of anywhere that dense shoals of baitfish gather such as around an old stone wall (many reservoirs,

remember, are flooded farmlands) or group of buildings, or the 'deeper' bed of a stream or river, rocky outcrops, defunct farm machinery, etc. The possibilities are endless, and all will show up on the finder.

19 Have you ever thought about fishing for pike at night? In some cases, particularly on waters heavily fished for pike, in both rivers and still waters, results can actually surpass those made during daylight. Dead baiting using simple ledgering tactics, presenting static baits on the bottom is by far the easiest and most productive method. Pretend you are carp fishing at night by using electric bite alarms and indicators, and by taking along hot drinks and warm clothing (if fishing in the depths of winter) plus a powerful torch and other necessities such as a towel and head lamp etc.

Actually pre-baiting during the hours of darkness, areas that are popular during the

day can make an enormous difference to your results. Try it and see.

20 Ever tried fly fishing for pike? I should say 'fly-rodding' really, because with pike, and to a much lesser extent other predatory species such as chub, perch and zander, flies are tied up to represent small fish, frogs, newts or small rodents, etc, not flying insects.

You need a fairly long (10 foot is ideal) powerful rod capable of throwing 9 and 10 weight lines, plus a large diameter fly reel, preferably with a sensitive disc drag. Add a floating, sinking and fast-sinking line, and you are there, but for a few short, supple wire traces (which become the leader tippet) plus an assortment of large flies and bugs. It's great fun too, and in shallow water especially, the turn of speed and subsequent tail-walking action from a fly-hooked pike can prove spectacular.

Roach & Dace

1 Being a shoal fish, roach are forever watchful of changing situations and circumstances that affect their brethren. Which is why the entire shoal often stops feeding confidently at the drop of a hat (as though a switch has been pulled) when danger occurs. Like the sudden appearance of a pike in the swim, with its fins quivering (a sure sign of its intention to attack) or simply the sun suddenly hitting clear water at an angle that immediately illuminates everything. The shoal is merely relating to its vulnerability.

This is why the biggest, wiliest roach of all, those over that magical 2lb bracket for instance, whose fellow shoal members have diminished in numbers over the seasons, through predation and disease, usually only feed with the utmost confidence in conditions of low light: at dusk and into darkness, and again at dawn. Because time has taught them they are far less vulnerable and subsequently less likely to be attacked and eaten, when their pursuers cannot see so well. A point well worth remembering.

2 When you cannot buy a bite from river roach in cold, winter conditions, it is because their metabolism has slowed down and they refuse to move quickly in order to intercept food on the move, no matter how juicy your maggots. Fact is, roach hate changing position every few seconds in really cold water and expending unnecessary energy. They much prefer to slowly suck up small particles of 'static'

Above: Tip 3

Centre: Tip 5

food such as maggots from the river bed. So switch over to quiver-tip ledgering, using a small block-end feeder (to deposit loose feed with extreme accuracy beside your hook bait) and offer two maggots on a size 16 hook, stepping down to smaller hooks and a single maggot if bites are not forthcoming.

3 Want a really big dace? Something between say, 12 ounces and that magical one pound figure. Then here's a good tip: concentrate trotting maggots or small cubes of bread crust, close to the bottom in the deeper, 'roachy-looking' swims of smaller rivers, particularly chalk streams, during the last two weeks of the river fishing season in early March. Dace are often segregated by sex at this time as an early grouping process prior to their eventual spawning during April, with the big, pigeon-chested females resting up in the deeper, slower swims, while the males, (already covered in spawning tubercles) decidedly wiry and sand-papery to hold, mass together along the fast, shallow reaches.

4 When ledgering using basic rigs with small baits presented on small hooks for roach and dace, particularly during the cold, winter months when bites are far less aggressive, it's imperative to employ the most sensitive of quiver-tip indicators. For those who do not own built-in, or push-in quiver tip rods of varying tip strengths, invest in a selection of screw-in quiver tips starting at one ounce test curve for really slow currents, going up

to 2-2½ ounces for rivers like the full-flowing Severn.

5 There is something extraordinarily satisfying about watching a strong flow whisk your red-topped float smoothly downstream. The current draws the 2lb-2½lb test line steadily from a free-running centre pin reel, while you gently brake the side of the drum with thumb pressure, ensuring the bait is presented as near as possible to the actual current speed down there close to the bottom. Yes, searching for specimen-sized roach in running water is arguably the most rewarding of all ways to see a big one come sliding over your net. And by big, lets say roach

of around 2lb and upwards, because being in a minority and rather scarce in these times of chronic 'cormorant predation', such fish are now extremely highly prized. And to encourage one to intercept a moving bait (maggots, casters or a piece of fresh white bread flake) mild conditions coupled to a 'coloured' river are imperative.

If long trotting, and the river's running crystal clear, you're unlikely to get a bite until the light fades, and then you have but a few casts remaining to score. But catch the river immediately following heavy flooding when visibility just starts to improve, but where you still lose sight of a maggot a foot below the surface, and those roach, if they exist in a large enough shoal, could well feed for at least a couple of hours. So make the most of mild spells and coloured water.

6 To alleviate the annoyance of debris, both surface and down the line, when ledgering for roach and dace in a swollen river, you have two options. Either to fish 'static' mill or over-shoot pools that have backed up – which can be 'full' of fish in the right conditions. Or, to select swims immediately behind wide bridge supports, behind sunken trees or on the inside and immediately downstream of acute bends. In short, wherever fish group up to seek respite out of the main flow, and where the full force of the current is deflected away from your ledgered bait.

7 To catch roach and dace using the 'waggler' float, it is important to bulk most of the shotting capacity (say 75-85 percent) on each side of the bottom ring, leaving a ½ inch gap between for the float to 'fold' smoothly on the strike. This not only allows 'dart-like' accuracy when casting because the shots pull the float through the air, but also only the very minimum of shots are then required 'down the line', to create a natural fall of the hook bait, which is most important when fishing in still waters.

This leaves you free to add just a few small shot (No 6 and 8 shot are perfect) starting midway between float and hook. Then, if the rig happens to 'fold' at the highest shot, the hook won't be able to touch the float or locking shots and tangle.

For trotting in running water, larger shots can be used down the line, and an overall 'heavier' bulk shotting in order that the bait trundles along close to or actually 'dragging' bottom.

8 Remember to have a 'peaked' base ball-type cap or visor in your kit when float fishing for roach and dace in bright conditions. It is essential to stop you from squinting all day when concentrating upon the float tip.

9 When 'waggler' fishing for roach in waters where you may need to change from straight to tipped or insert floats, or to models carrying a greater shotting load, or maybe you simply wish to switch from a red top to a black top for 'silhouette' situations, attach the float to your line using a silicon float adaptor. Switching from one float to another then takes seconds.

10 When you're float fishing or ledgering for roach and dace and your maggots or casters repeatedly come back 'crushed', you have actually missed and perhaps not even seen, a 'positive' bite. All cyprinid species including roach and dace are equipped with powerful 'pharyngeal' teeth in the back of their throats, for masticating their food, and so

to wind in 'sucked maggots' means the fish has actually had your hook well inside its mouth.

To remedy this so you can identify a bite, keep shortening your hook tail if ledgering, or if float fishing move the lowest shot closer to the hook till bites are registered. Also, (and this is imperative in cold conditions) shoot the float tip down so it's a mere 'blimp' in the surface film.

11 When ledgering for roach and dace in fast flowing rivers during the cold winter months using a block-end feeder rig, and you don't want maggots or casters emptying too quickly, here's a useful tip. Keep a roll of black electrician's tape in your kit, so you can slow down the rate of release by taping up some of the holes. Simple, but effective.

12 Regardless of which type of feeder you start the day with, make sure it is attached to your lead-link via a tiny snap link swivel. Then you can change the size and type of your feeder, literally within seconds.

13 When using bread flake on the hook do not pinch it on 'too' hard, especially when long trotting, otherwise hook penetration at distance becomes a problem. Pinch only a small area of the flake (around the eye of the

Above: Tip 11

hook) on hard, allowing the rest to swell into an attractive 'carnation' around the hook.

14 For 'quiver-tip' ledgering at night, here is one easy way of watching a powerful 'beta light' element, or one of the extra-bright 'chemical luminous elements', both of which can be sleeved into a short length of clear tubing pushed onto a 'Tip-sight' holder which itself is sleeved into silicon tubing on the quiver tip immediately below the tip ring. First of all a length of clear silicone tubing is sleeved over the tiny tip ring to accommodate the holder. For a more permanent fixture, the holder may be whipped to the quiver tip.

15 An even easier way of adding a 'luminous' element for night fishing, is by attaching an 'Enterprise

Tackle' nightlight adaptor. This ingenious piece of kit which can literally be fitted in seconds, accommodates elements between 3.0 and 4.5mm in diameter in a short length of clear tubing and keeps the two halves of the unit (which actually 'hinges and folds around the quiver tip) held tightly together. These adaptors come two to a packet, one large and one small. The larger will also fit on rod tops up to 2mm in diameter.

16 If luminous elements fail to hold your attention for ledgering at night, then simply illuminate a 'white-painted' quiver tip or rod top with a narrow torch beam. Position it from downstream, to angle outwards and upstream, thus illuminating 'only' the quiver tip. It will then not impair your night-time vision, nor shine into the water and scare the fish.

17 To quickly construct a mini ledger, pinch a shot onto the line 10-18 inches above the hook, and immediately above fold a short length of 'slightly thicker line' over the reel line. Pinch onto this sufficient shots to hold bottom, leaving a gap slightly narrower than the stop shot, so the ledger slides freely up the line.

18 To fish the 'stick float' correctly, you need calm conditions, (a gentle upstream wind is sometimes advantageous) and all the shots should be evenly spaced (shirt-button style) between float and hook. For the most subtle presentation of small baits like a single maggot or caster, make the two shots closest to the hook smaller than the rest. See Diagram. The stick float works most effectively in depths from 4-10 feet, but only at short range with the tip dotted down to a mere 'blimp' in the surface film, if held back gently when being run through, so fish it no further out than an under arm flick. A rod length and a half out, say.

Right: Tip 18

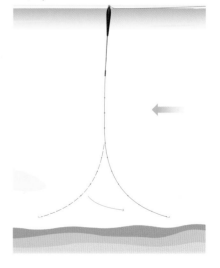

Left: Tip 19

Do not allow any loose line between rod and float tip and get used to counting down and observing how many seconds it takes for all the shots to dot the tip of the float down to its final position, and strike instantly when it takes too long. One big shot may very well cock the same float instantly, but up to a dozen tiny shots will take several seconds, and this is your period for interpreting and striking into bites on the drop.

19 Of course not all bites will come on the drop when fishing the stick float. Some will occur when the float is allowed to run through totally unchecked and actually preceding the bait. Holding back steadily however will encourage the bait to fish almost directly beneath the float, thus instantly indicating the tiniest of bites from the wiliest big roach or dace. Those who trot using a centre pin reel and brake the line by applying gentle thumb pressure to the reels drum, enjoy superb control for easing a stick float downstream. There is in fact no finer reel to use for this technique.

20 To locate big roach in our smaller, richest rivers, walk the river at dawn and again at dusk with binoculars. Even during the colder winter months big roach love to porpoise on the surface, especially during those frosty mornings, instantly giving away the whereabouts of the shoal, which tend to occupy the same, even-paced runs and glides all winter through. Seeing that large, red dorsal fin, followed by a red tail as the roach rolls is a lovely and quite unmistakable sight.

Rudd &
Golden Orfe

Centre: Tip 4

1 Although most anglers tend to associate catching rudd with offering free-falling baits close to the surface during the summer months, in shallow lakes averaging 3-6 feet which tend to warm up quickly during mild winter spells, estate lakes in particular, rudd, and large rudd at that, are a very targetable species.

2 For 'winter rudd' try at the deepest end of an estate lake (close to the dam) and put out a dozen or so tangerine-sized balls of bread-based ground bait at a short to medium casting distance. Say 30 to 50 yards out from the dam. Then, using a two-rod ledgering approach (Avon style rods are ideal for the job) simply ledger thumbnail-sized lumps of fresh white bread flake covering size 10-8 hooks tied

direct to a 4lbs reel line.

3 For bite indication when ledgering for rudd, and this applies both summer or winter, rely on simple 'bobbin-type' indicators, and whilst many bites will give positive 'lifts' or 'drops' of the bobbin, don't be afraid of striking at 'two-inch' movements. Fishing lighter with smaller baits will only attract 'smaller' Rudd. And you could be looking at beautiful golden-sided specimens close to or even exceeding 2lbs. So don't settle for less.

4 Whilst rudd regularly hybridize with roach wherever both species occur, only rarely in England do rudd/bream hybrids (they are common in Southern Ireland) exist. Rudd/bream hybrids are actually a fine, hard fighting fish displaying the finer qualities of both species. They are thick-set with muted, golden-bronze flanks (quite unlike any other fish) and have scales noticeably larger than a true bream. The fins however are red-brown and the lips usually level.

5 Catching rudd on the fly rod during the warm summer months when they cavort regularly on the surface in the pursuit of hatching flies is a true delight. An 8 or 9 foot 4-weight outfit with floating line and a fine leader tapering to just a 2-3lbs tippet is perfect for the job and allows rudd of all sizes to show their sporting value. By their splashes, identify whether fish are sucking down adult insects on the surface or insects emerging from their pupas in the surface film and match your artificial accordingly.

6 Good patterns of dry flies to tempt rudd are black gnat, (which represents many adult midges), all the olives and particularly small sedges. They will also move aggressively to lightly

leaded imitations presented 'on the drop' such as a mayfly nymph or a shrimp pattern, when nothing is happening on the surface.

7 Targeting rudd that are feeding close to or actually from the surface is most effectively practiced using the 'flat-float' controller technique. The 'controller' which adds both weight for casting in addition to a visual indicator, is simply a 2-5 inch length of unpainted peacock quill (what could be more natural floating flat on the surface than a

bird quill) common reed, or (for fishing at greater distances) 1/3rd of an inch diameter stained, (use green garden fence stain) hardwood dowel. Each of these three floats is attached to the reel line with a wide band of silicone rubber at each end, 2-6 foot above the hook, with a shot close up to each end.

8 Using a heavier 'dowel' controller, additional casting weight is usually not required. But for peacock quill and reed, simply pinch a BB or AA shot onto the line at each end. Surprising distances can be cast

with flat controllers, using naturally buoyant baits like casters, bread crust, or pellets presented in the surface film. Alternatively, a crust and bread flake cocktail, or a caster and maggot cocktail, etc can be offered 'on the drop'. Gloriously 'positive' bites result from fishing the flat float technique, with it suddenly sliding across the surface or actually being dragged under. So hold the rod throughout.

9 A lightweight, 13-14 foot 'waggler' rod coupled to a baby fixed spool reel filled with clear, 3lbs test mono, is the perfect combo for surface rudd fishing. And you'll need a catapult for regularly putting out floating casters way up wind to get the rudd up on the surface and active.

10 For taking rudd off the top at long distance (30 yards plus) swap the 'flat-floats' for a small 'tenpin' floating controller, stopped by a five turn stop knot and tiny rubber bead, 2-4 foot above the hook. For catching carp/rudd off the top, see Carp Tip 4.

11 To distinguish between a true rudd and a roach/rudd hybrid

RUDD & GOLDEN ORFE

Below: Tip 12

first look at the fish's lips. The true rudd has a noticeably protruding lower jaw, showing it was purpose built for feeding effectively near the surface, while with 'hybrids' the lips could be level.

The body of a true rudd is noticeably deeper than that of either a 'hybrid' or roach and the colour is of burnished, highly reflective, buttery-gold enamel along the flanks, fusing upwards into olive-bronze along the back. Its fins are bright orange-scarlet, and there is a distinct 'keel' to the anal fin, which is overlapped in a vertical line by the dorsal. 'Hybrids' are of a more even, muted, far less intense colouration. So if you are in any doubt on any of the above counts about the fish you have just caught, discount it as a true rudd. For rudd/bream 'hybrids' see Tip 4.

12 To stand a chance of catching numbers of specimen-sized

rudd (fish between two and three pounds) which by the year are becoming less common in England, Ireland, in both the north and the south, throughout its canal, river and inter connecting lake-land waterways, offers superlative rudd fishing. Contact The Irish Tourist Board, or top Tour Operator like Anglers World Holidays, tel 01246 221717.

13 In lakes and pits where carp, tench or bream predominate, species at the end of the food chain like rudd, especially big rudd, are at their most catchable when the other species are not. So concentrate on locating the rudd shoals during the middle of the day when they love to bask close to the surface.

14 Big rudd also feed in earnest at dusk and dawn, giving away their whereabouts by cavorting and porpoising in the surface film as they inhale emerging insects. They can however at such times be encouraged to accept large bottom baits such as a thumbnail-sized piece of bread flake covering a size 8 hook (rudd have large mouths) ledgered over a few handfuls of mashed bread ground bait. But once fish start disappearing from the shoal

Above: Tip 15

sport is often short-lived.

15 Like roach, rudd are covered in protective mucus which is easily removed by holding them in dry hands. So always wet your hands (quickly grabbing the wet landing net mesh will do) before picking one up to unhook.

16 Rudd are equipped, as are all cyprinids from gudgeon to the mighty mahseer, with a pair of powerful 'pharyngeal (throat) teeth' for masticating their natural food into a pulp prior to swallowing. Which

Far Right: Tip 19

is why worm or maggot baits often come back 'crushed', when you have either missed or not even seen a bite, but your hook must have been sucked back into the fish's throat just the same.

17 To remedy missed or unregistered bites from rudd, either shorten your hook length if ledgering, or move the bottom shot much closer to the hook if float fishing.

18 For targeting small groups of big rudd which are loath to leave the sanctuary of lily pads during daylight, 'free lining' a slow-sinking bait 'on the drop' often scores where 'static', bottom-fished baits do not. Try a large piece of fresh white bread flake, 'lightly' pinched onto a size 10 or 8 hook, so that upon landing on the surface it very slowly descends. Experiment in the margins to ascertain exactly how hard you need to pinch the bread on so it sinks slowly, before casting amongst the lilies. And then watch the line like a hawk as the bread slowly sinks, striking instantly into any unusual movement. Fortunately, rudd amongst lilies are invariably bold biters, with the line fair 'zinging tight' or dramatically 'falling slack', should a

fish swim towards the rod.

19 Golden orfe are not dissimilar to rudd in that they are always on the move, darting about and forever looking upwards in order to intercept 'falling' food items, or one floating on the surface. And everything mentioned in Tips, 7, 8 and 10 for catching rudd, will also account for the beautifully coloured golden orfe.

20 Golden rudd, are quite a rarity in fisheries, although they are a popular pond fish. Their overall 'salmon-pink' colouration is much like the golden orfe, and they are no different to catch than naturally coloured rudd. Because of their bright and distinct colour they feed quickly when close to the surface. It's almost as though they realize that they are brightly coloured and thus an easy target to predatory birds like the heron and of course pike. One reason perhaps, why it is that whenever golden rudd are stocked into a fishery with naturally coloured rudd, with which they interbreed freely, incidentally, they never seem to last too long. They are simply too visible to predators like albino fish.

Tench

1 To help 'dour' tench fishing come 'alive', try actually wading into shallow, weedy swims (wearing chest-high waders of course) and with a long handled garden rake give the bottom detritus a really good going over whilst creating (if the weed is that bad) a wide channel to fish in. In less than a hour's work (there is nothing to stop you preparing two or three spots) a swim can be cleared and the bottom subsequently stirred up with all manner of natural food items left in suspension ready for the tench to turn up in a hungry mood. Which they will do quicker than you can imagine with colour in the water. For deep swims, purchase one of those wide, heavy rake heads to which rope can be tied for throwing out.

2 Learning to understand the distinctive 'feeding' bubbles of tench will result in more fish in your net. Small clusters of say four to ten small, non-fizzy bubbles rising to the surface come from the fish itself, (through its gills in fact) which is what happens when all cyprinid species masticate their food with their powerful 'pharyngeal' (throat) teeth. Whereas those long lines or patches of larger, 'fizzy' bubbles come from 'methane' trapped immediately below the bottom detritus rising to the surface. You can sometimes actually see bits of twigs and leaves accompanying bubbles into the surface film. The result of vegetation such as leaves and weed that has rotted

Above: Tip 4

down, and subsequently been released by a tench standing on its nose and deliberately running along the bottom to dislodge items of natural food such as shrimps and bloodworms, etc.

3 To duplicate the kind of 'fizzy' bubbles tench send up via the bottom detritus when feeding aggressively, just run a rod rest or the end of your landing net handle along the bottom of any 'silty' swim, especially those directly beneath trees and you will immediately create the same effect.

4 When fishing at 'close range' float fishing the 'lift method' is phenomenally successful due to the way species like tench (also crucian carp, and

to a lesser extent bream and king carp) feed naturally, by standing on their heads to suck up baits from the bottom. By using a slim stem of 'buoyant' peacock quill (waggler float) attached with silicon tubing at the bottom end only, which not only 'lifts' (hence the method's name) but actually supports a single large shot fixed on the line 3-5 inches from the bait, during the time it takes the tench to right itself back into to a horizontal position, a firm strike can be made at any time before the float actually lies flat. Once it does, the tench is of course supporting the shot and may eject the bait. So never wait for the float to go under before striking. This applies to all species targeted with the 'lift-method'. See Diagram.

5 Unlike most cyprinids, male and female tench can be told apart easier than any other species. The smaller, often darker, more 'dogged-fighting' males have crinkly, spoon-shaped pelvic fins which when spread out cover the anal vent, with lumpy, protruding muscles or gonads above. Whilst the pelvic fins of the female are smooth, of normal shape and do not cover the vent.

6 To facilitate quick and easy attachment of 'bobbin' indicators to your bank sticks when ledgering for tench, simply

whip on a tiny rod ring at the top of the bank stick. Then add a snap-link swivel to the end of your 'bobbin' retaining line. Incidentally, a two foot length of 80lbs test Dacron is the perfect material for 'bobbin' retaining lines. Possessing minimal stretch it will not 'twang' back like heavy monofilament on the strike.

7 In summer lakes which have a covering of filamentous weed on the bottom, tench really respond to ledgered baits that are popped-up just above the weed and in plain view. Try baiting with a large lobworm and inject a little air into the head end, fixing a

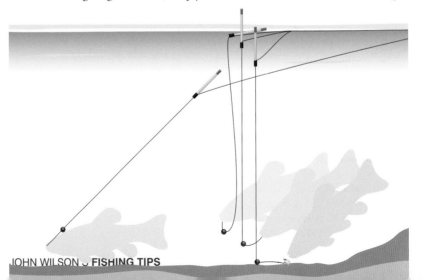

large shot on the line several inches from the worm so it floats up just above the weed in an attractive, gyrating manner. Alternatively, try a cube of luncheon meat on a hair, to which a piece of buoyant rig foam (cut to the same width of the meat) has been added. Make sure this is threaded on last so it floats uppermost.

8 If when ledgering for tench using small hooks and maggots the maggots come back 'crushed', (indicating they have in fact been sucked back to the fish's pharyngeal teeth for mastication) keep reducing your hook (shorter and shorter) length till 'hittable' bites are registered on

your indicator. Alternatively, keep your eyes glued to the line where it goes into the water immediately in front of the rod tip, and strike at any lift or twitch, no matter how slight.

9 To counteract subsurface tow when ledgering for tench using 'bobbin-type' indicators such as the 'Tenpin', simply pinch one or two 2, or 3x SSG shots onto the retaining line immediately below the bobbin.

10 Wherever clear water tench are unbelievably 'spooky' during the hours of daylight, float fishing at night using a luminous 'chemical-element' tip which is sleeved onto a waggler-style

float via a piece of clear tubing, is often the answer. Bites not only happen, as the light starts to fade, but are most positive. The 'lift-Method' works well here. See Tip 4.

11 There is no favourite or best method for coming to grips with the rare, 'golden tench'. This beautiful creature, with a 'black eye' often called 'banana fish' due to its bright yellowy, sometimes orangey body, flecked all over with small black markings, (just like

a banana) appears not to hybridize with the common green tench, and exists in only a few isolated fisheries within the British Isles.

12 If you wish to specifically target a rare golden tench, then visit the complex of lakes at the 'Anglers Paradise' fishery in Devon, which contain good numbers of this breath-taking species to 7lbs plus.

13 When casting tight up to reed lines from the bank or an

Above: Tip 13

Far Left: Tip 11

anchored punt or boat (surely one of the nicest ways of accounting for summer tench) use a bodied waggler float rig with most of the bulk shot grouped around the base (which precedes the bait during the cast) and have just two small shots down the line, the lowest 6-8 inches from the hook actually coming to rest on the bottom once the bait has 'arced' downwards through the water to settle immediately below the float, mere inches from the reed stems along which tench patrol.

14 Ledgering 'method-feeder' style is a deadly way of taking summer tench, especially from distant swims. Use a ground bait mix that breaks down quickly (it's no good lying there clogged around the frame feeder for 30 minutes when tench are on the rampage) and use a short 4-6 inch hook length. Include hook bait samples like casters, chopped worm, corn or small feed pellets in your ground bait mix, whilst baiting with the same on the hook.

15 To complement a pellet-based feeder ground bait, soft hook pellets are especially effective whether hair rigged or side hooked. Alternatively, and this works great over filamentous bottom weed, hair

rig artificial floating sweet corn, which floats up above the weed. Tench hit it like it's the only kernel of corn left in the lake. Artificial casters can score too.

16 Free-lining for tench may well seem an ancient technique in these days of hair-rigging and bolt rigs, but in certain situations it can still produce. Tench hugging the margins amongst reed mace or sedges for instance or those lying beneath the shade of overhanging rhododendron bushes or willows, where a heavy bolt lead rig 'sploshed' in amongst them, will put an instant end to any possible result. Tench moving through gaps in dense weed immediately below the rod tip, or simply tench moving very close in through clear water that can be easily seen and cast to.

17 In each of the above situations, free lined bait, especially a 'natural' bait like a big lobworm, is liable to be immediately inhaled without suspicion. Or you could try a large piece of soft protein paste, a piece of 'slow-sinking' bread flake, or better still a bait of 'balanced' paste and crust that will come to rest on top of the most dense weed.

18 To free line effectively you need to be nicely camouflaged

Far Left: Tip 14

and kneeling or sitting well back from the water's edge so that only the end of your rod hangs out over the surface along the margins. You then simply watch the fish or the line between surface and rod tip for bites, and you'll enjoy the most glorious of uninhibited 'slow' indications, where you can almost pre-empt the line lifting and snaking out behind the tench as it moves away with your bait, before striking firmly. And what fights and long runs you'll enjoy as a consequence! So use an Avon type rod and just a 6lbs reel line with a number 6 hook tied direct.

19 When 'immediate' bites are expected to a free lined bait, simply hook your forefinger around the line just above the bale arm, so that you'll still feel the line move should your attentions be elsewhere.

20 For long free lining sessions rig up both front and rear rod rests with the rod tip angled downwards, and loop a coil of silver kitchen foil around the line between reel and butt ring on a two foot drop. Fish with a closed bale arm so you can strike the instant the foil indicator either rises or drops back.

Trout

1 When sight-casting to monster rainbows and the big browns especially, of small exceptionally clear-watered, man made lakes, and they won't play ball, showing not the slightest interest in a sumptuous, weighted, slow falling imitative nymph no matter how attractively you 'twitch' it, try this. Observe closely the 'movement route' of the particular trout you're after (most big, small-water trout adopt a 'favoured' feeding route) and select an area where it usually comes close and is thus easily visible through the clear depths. Now, with your prize trout well out of sight, roll out a heavily weighted Czech nymph of a colour you can clearly see, tied to a long leader and allow it to free fall down to the bottom, obviously at a spot over which the trout will eventually pass. Keep your eyes glued to the exact spot and when the fish next comes round, twitch your Czech nymph up off the bottom clearly within its path. Bingo!

2 For an entirely 'different' slant on modern fly fishing for trout, which is really great fun, why not try 'float-tubing'? Many lake-land and reservoir trout fishery complexes up and down the country encourage this fascinating approach and even have equipment for hire. If you already own a set of diving fins and lightweight, chest-high waders however, you may even wish to purchase your own 'tube'.

3 To enjoy a days 'tubing' you simply walk backwards into the water (fins/ flippers already on) with shoulder straps supporting the tube which has an open front, across which is stretched a webbing seat, and suddenly you're afloat, sitting most comfortably with legs dangling ready to work those fins. Most purpose-built tubes have zipped compartments on top to house necessities, and can be easily inflated (built-in tubes for blowing into) and deflated in minutes. You get to explore all those awkward to fish (from bank or boat), tree-covered spots around islands, etc and there is a wonderful sense of 'freedom' when out tubing. And subsequently playing fish when actually 'in' the water is pure joy.

4 Fancy some action with jet propelled rainbows and maybe even the occasional big brown or two during the cold winter months? It's fabulous fun! Gone, for some thank goodness, are the days when fly fishers packed away their rods throughout the winter because trout were perpetuating their spawning cycle, and hooking into skinny black cock fish with kype-like jaws, or gravid hen fish swollen with roe, was just not on.

Today however, progressive still water fisheries stock only with 'triploids', trout coming from eggs that have been subjected to a heat-shock treatment, making them 'sexless' adults which remain in tip top 'silver' condition all year round, and fighting fit, using all their

energy packing on weight as opposed to producing eggs or milt.

5 And how do triploids fight in cold water conditions? If anything they actually battle harder and for considerably longer during the winter, particularly in deep, clear, still water fisheries. So what's stopping you?

6 Though individually 'small' in size, the family of 'midges' which we fly fishermen refer to as 'buzzers' (because the hordes of egg-carrying females when gyrating over the water at head height audibly 'buzz') includes more than 400 species, and is easily the most important family of flies for the still water angler. But really, just a couple of imitations, say black and red standard buzzer patterns, and the same again in 'suspender' or 'emerger' versions, where flotation fibres at their heads (to represent gills on the naturals) suspend them in the surface film, with their bodies hanging vertically, are all the fly fisherman needs to fool most trout.

7 The midge larva, non other than the 'bloodworm' is arguably one of, if not 'the' most prolific and thus the most valuable source of natural food not only for trout, but for all our cyprinid species too, from rudd to the largest carp.

8 When out boat fishing huge expanses of still water like reservoirs, and fish are on 'buzzers', but due to bright conditions the trout are staying deep, the standard technique of 'drift fishing' does not always work. This is because by the time you have cast out and let the team of flies sink to the right depth before starting the retrieve, the cast is almost back to the boat and you have to recast. Far better therefore to anchor-up and let the flies sink to the required depth, then make the retrieve at your own pace.

9 Barometric pressure is something we all 'know' must seriously affect our sport, but rarely get to pin point when.

Well, those who regularly fish small, man made, clear water trout fisheries where trout can be clearly seen repeatedly refusing whatever fly is put before them, have noticed that the trout's mood changes 'drastically' in line with a change in barometric pressure. Whereupon they suddenly snap at anything for a few casts, before going back to being difficult again. And those whose wrist watch shows that pressure change, have subsequently bagged up. Food for thought, eh?

10 For catching 'cold water trout' in the early spring which are stocked into the deep water of reservoirs and gravel-pit fisheries where depths might

Far Right: Tip 16

shelve to 30 feet plus, then presenting a 'booby' fished on a short 3-5 foot leader and Hi-D, ultra fast sinking line, is one hell of an effective way of turning a 'hopeless' day into success.

11 'Boobies' are so effective because they work in reverse to all other flies. When you start to retrieve, having allowed enough time for much of your Hi-D line to be laying on the bottom, 'boobies' (so named for the two extra 'buoyant' polystyrene balls - breasts no less) tied around the hook, will angle sharply 'downwards' as opposed to 'upwards' like all other artificials. So even the most wily, and fished-for trout has not the slightest reservation in gobbling them up. Most fish are in fact hooked way back in the throat.

12 If purchasing your first 'priest' for dispatching your catch quickly, then select one where one end unscrews and 'reverses' to become a 'marrow spoon' which when sleeved down the trout's throat and into the top of its stomach, will, after pressing its belly gently, tell you exactly what insects it has been feeding upon, so that you can match your artificial to the natural.

13 To obtain the utmost enjoyment from catching trout, particularly large rainbows, from still water fisheries, invest in a specialized 'smoker' which via a small metholated spirit burner heating hardwood, aromatic sawdust placed on top of the heating plate, cures, cooks and hot smokes your catch all in one. Try putting the hot-smoked flank of a large trout, wrapped in silver foil together with a large knob of butter and masses of coarse-ground black pepper, onto the Bar-B-Q. Lovely!

14 When casting a fly, always wear a hat, preferably one with a peak to alleviate glare and concentrate your field of vision (shield your eyes with your hand as if looking into the sun and you will see what I mean) plus 'Polarized' glasses. Together they greatly reduce the painful experience of a fly, travelling over 50 miles an hour, embedding in your head, or worse still, an eye.

15 If fly fishing from the bank, it makes more sense to spread your fly collection around your waistcoat in a number of small boxes, each holding different patterns such as nymphs, lures, dry flies, emergers,

buzzers, and so on, as opposed to one large (wooden) box, favoured by many reservoir boat anglers . Upon leaving the car, you can then set off with exactly the types and patterns of flies that might be required during your day's fishing, instead of carting the kitchen sink, and its dog around.

16 Endeavour, even if it's only once in your lifetime, to be beside a top chalk stream trout fishery (to hell with the expense) with rod in hand, at 'Mayfly' time. The thickest 'hatches' of this extraordinary aquatic insect usually occur during the last couple of weeks in May, (global warming accepted) and trout gorge themselves silly. After getting your hand in with a couple or three 'easy' fish, you'll know whether trout are showing a preference for the newly-hatched fly or spent insects lying on the surface, inert with their wings stretched out. You can then take time in stalking one of those 'whopper' brown trout that only ever seem to present any chance of them sucking down an artificial, during the 'Mayfly' cycle.

17 For fly fishing all day in both large and small sheets of still

**Centre Left &
Right:** Tip 18

water, without the undue fatigue of continually bringing your rod back and forwards, back and forwards, in order to get a long line out, learn the art of 'double-haul' casting. This entails roll casting, say a third of your line forwards, (following the retrieve) and momentarily pulling hard on the line during the back cast to accelerate its flight. A second downwards pull or 'haul' is then made (with your hand gripping the line immediately below the butt ring) prior to making the forward cast. And this acceleration will shoot out whatever line you have on the ground. It is in fact easier to do than explain because it's mostly all down to feel and timing. But turning round to watch the flight of your back cast will help enormously. And remember that the line must be as straight in the air as possible at the beginning of each 'haul' whether forwards or backwards. Try it.

18 Both 'golden' and 'blue' rainbow trout are not different species, merely coloured variants of the rainbow trout, whereas, a 'brown bow', is a sterile hybrid (little bred by fish farmers these days) resulting from the crossing of a rainbow with a brown

trout. The 'cheetah' is another sterile hybrid, resulting from the crossing of a rainbow with an American brook trout. And the 'tiger' is a sterile hybrid resulting from the crossing of an American brook trout with a brown trout. Incidentally, only into a handful of 'southern' chalk-stream fed lakes are any of these colourful trout stocked nowadays.

19 Never set out across a trout reservoir for a day's fly fishing without a 'drogue', which is employed in windy conditions to slow down the boat's drift so that you have more control over the way your flies are fishing.

20 One of the most delightful ways of catching reservoir trout is to drift 'loch style', casting ahead of the drifting boat set sideways-on to the wind (with a drogue over the windward side) into the relatively 'calm' surface of 'wind lanes'. Long casts are generally made down a particular lane, and a team of three flies steadily retrieved back to the boat. Watch out for rainbows especially, which at the last second just as you start the backwards cast, appear from nowhere to shoot up and grab the point fly or sometimes even the' bob'.

Salmon & Sea Trout

1 Fancy catching a salmon on a 5 or 6 weight trout, brook-rod, and a leader tapered to just 6lbs test? Well, it is certainly not impossible, and guaranteed fun. You just need a little confidence and of course access to smallish clear-flowing rivers where salmon are known to rest up fairly close into the bank, because 'casting' is not in any order of importance here. The secret, having identified a lie close into the bank likely to hold a fish or two, immediately downstream from a croy, or beside pilings or behind a 'salmon stone' is to let a really heavily weighted nymph (a gold head for instance) quickly reach bottom following a short roll cast made square

on, and then 'lift' it steadily upwards to the surface, where, every so often, a salmon, having followed it up through sheer curiosity, will nail it just before, or actually on the top. Sounds strange I know, but the technique really works well on small rivers, particularly southern chalk streams.

2 Selecting the right artificial to tempt Atlantic salmon that are periodically stocked into still water trout fisheries, is almost an impossibility. These particular 'oddities' do seem to feed on natural food items, and strangely, do not 'colour up' as might be expected, even when still uncaught in a lake for a year or more. A trait they do follow

easier, than with a fixed spool reel.

Centre: Tip 1

Start by casting directly across the flow and once the spoon touches bottom, simply put the reel back into gear and, holding the rod tip up, allow the current to bounce and wobble the spoon slowly across the river, occasionally touching bottom. Do not attempt to retrieve as the spoon comes around or it will rise and work too fast for a salmon to grab hold. It pays to have amongst your kit several different weights (from say 12 to 28, even 40 grams) of the same colour spoon, to work varying depths and current speeds.

4 When the lure reaches the end of its downstream ark and starts to 'dangle' just like a fly, then, and only then, start a slow retrieve. Then, when the spoon is back at the rod, take a short pace downstream and repeat the cast. In wide rivers make two casts at each spot before moving. The first short and the second long, to cover all potential lies.

5 One of the most famous salmon and sea trout lures, the 'Devon minnow' can really produce in cold water conditions. It is offered in the traditional, 'downstream and across'

however is that even in large lakes they seem to favour definite 'patrol routes' which take them close into the bank, similar to the characteristics of large brown trout. So it's not so much the fly offered, but where and at what depth. Something that can actually be visually worked out in clear water fisheries.

3 When using 'Toby-type' spoons for catching salmon, a 'multiplier outfit' (6501 or 7001 sized left-hand wind) not only fits snugly into your hand (go for a 'trigger-grip' reel fitting, behind which your forefinger sits comfortably) counting the lure down to the river bed before clicking the reel back into gear is so much

catches plenty of sea trout and salmon too.

7 To cover runs or pools that can only be approached from downstream, one lure tops all others. So don't go salmon or sea trout fishing anywhere without a few 'Flying Condoms' in your kit. Referred to more reverently as the 'Flying C', which is really an elongated Mepp's-type spinner with a long, heavy, shaft and treble hook, over which is sleeved a coloured rubber tube, this lure works at its most effective when cast directly upstream and across. After touching bottom, it is then retrieved downstream and across with the flow. A technique which gives both salmon and sea trout a much shorter period of indecision, due to the angle and reduced length of time at which the lure cuts across their field of vision. And for this reason, the Flying C can prove deadly.

8 During the summer and autumn, long trotting for salmon in many of our smaller rivers, using a centre pin reel and a preserved shrimp presented attractively beneath a wide-topped float, will account for fish holding station in awkward, weedy, even impossible lies, which cannot

technique, either with a banana-shaped 'Wye' lead built into the trace 3 feet above the lure, which bounces over a rocky bottom, or presented on a separate 3 foot link joined to a three way swivel, below which is a 1-2 foot mono link and bomb, or stick weight that literally 'bounce' over the river bed. A buoyant, balsa wood Devon, will then spin well above any snags. It's always worth keeping a few different patterns in your waistcoat.

6 In Sweden, a similar rig to the latter method is used in conjunction not with lures, but large tube flies. It

110

JOHN WILSON'S **FISHING TIPS**

Left: Tip 7

be covered with the fly. Rig up an Avon-style rod with an 8-10lbs test reel line and a 'chubber' float carrying 4-5 SSG shots. Bulk this 18 inches above a size 8 treble hook with a 1½ -2 inch 'shrimping pin' threaded onto the line in between, so that it can be sleeved through the bait to keep it straight before nicking the treble into the head.

9 To present the preserved shrimp attractively, set the float to work the bait 1-2 feet above the river bed, and trot through at current pace, 'holding back' on the float every so often so the bait rises up attractively. And expect 'bold' bites, as though you were trotting for chub.

10 For joining a full line or a shooting head to braided backing, use the standard 'needle'

knot. See Diagram.

11 There is no doubt, especially in low and clear water conditions, that fly fishing for sea trout throughout the hours of darkness, vastly improves your chances of hooking up. But even shallow, intimate, little rivers take on an entirely different character at

Left: Tip 10

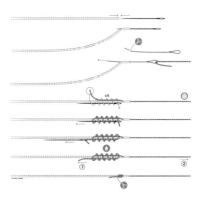

Right: Tip 13

night. So before you set forth into the night, walk your river slowly during daylight taking account of where trees and bushes are situated along each of the pools you intend covering and actually wade in to roughly where you will stand to cast. Take a good look all around on the bottom for large boulders or tree stumps that might trip you up and work out your casting angles required to move steadily along the pool, taking into account that fish will often not be so far away under the cloak of darkness.

12 When tackling sea trout at night be certain that everything you might need, from a small torch to a pair of scissors, spare tippet material to a small pair of forceps, plus your fly boxes, etc, are all stored and easily got at within the pockets of your waistcoat or wading vest. Realizing that your favourite flies are in a tackle bag back in the car when half way down a promising pool in the pitch black, is no laughing matter.

13 When tackling big, fast and boulder-strewn rivers for salmon or sea trout, where wading deeper than your knees, maybe up past your waist, is imperative to work yourself into a casting position for covering some pools, do not leave the bank without a 'heavy' wading staff,

Left: Tip 14

that is retained around your shoulders on a lanyard. You can then 'feel' your way downriver.

14 A pair of good quality, breathable, or neoprene chest high waders is an indispensable piece of kit to all salmon and sea trout fisherman, whether they Spey cast or throw artificial lures. To alleviate slipping on algae-covered stones and rocks and risk a ducking in freezing cold water, wading boots, which are worn over the integral neoprene socks, should have felt soles, as should waders with integral rubber boots. For really cold 'spring' conditions, 'all neoprene' waders' 5-6mm thick with integral,

felt soled boots are recommended.

15 One important thing to remember about Spey casting is to always allow the 'bow' in the D to fully form and hang beside you, before roll-casting the fly out. It's then so easy.

16 Here's a handy tip that I picked up at the famous 'junction beat' on Scotland's River Tweed when Spey casting for salmon. Once you have cast downstream and across and rolled an upstream loop in the line to 'mend' it, whilst holding the rod parallel with and low to the water as the line swings round, try moving the rod back say nine or ten inches, every few seconds,

river systems within the British Isles, should you not wish to eat your catch, do not even attempt to net or especially, handle it. Using a pair of long-nosed artery forceps, slip the hook free whilst it is lying beaten on its side, and take great pleasure in watching it swim off.

19 If you are ever unsure about whether you have caught a salmon or a sea trout, or indeed a giant brown trout, grip firmly around its tail root. Salmon have a narrow tail root often referred to as a 'wrist', with a ridged and distinct 'keel' to their tail and so can easily be lifted up. Whereas both brown and sea trout (one and the same animal really) have 'soft' tail edges, against which your hand will slip. So they cannot be easily lifted.

20 'Worming' or 'prawn' fishing for salmon work when other methods do not, and especially in difficult times, such as the river being heavily coloured and out of sorts. So do not be put off by the stigma that some game fishermen like to attach to 'bait fishing'. A salmon does not fight any the less for being hooked on bait. It's down to how you value that fight.

which moves the fly attractively at the other end in short surges. It induces takes on days when the fish are not really having it. Try it and see.

17 Remember that the exact height of a river will have a great influence on the chances of catching, whether fly fishing or working artificials. Ideally, a steadily falling river with the water clearing after a flood is most likely to induce salmon to lie-up in the pools for longer periods. Moreover, with the previous occupants nearly all having migrated upstream during the last spate, most fish in each pool will be newcomers and likely to hit the first angler's offering they see.

18 In these days of diminishing salmon returns from most

Zander

1 Zander are arguably, more sensitive to resistance, than any other British freshwater species. So when ledgering live or dead baits opt for a lightweight 'bobbin' indicator (that clip onto the line between reel and butt ring) hung on a two foot drop, as opposed to 'drop-off' indicators, which require significantly more pressure on behalf of the fish to register an indication. There are days when this makes all the difference between runs developing, and the bait being repeatedly dropped.

2 Even in heavily coloured water with mere 'inches' of visibility you can enjoy hectic sport with zander. Their large, light-reflecting

eyes are purpose built for hunting in low light conditions when the eyes of their prey, such as small roach, rudd, dace and bleak, are not. Try working a 3-5 inch freshly killed bleak up and down 'sink and draw' style, close to the bottom mounted on a double treble trace. The most successful of all rigs being the 'Drachkovitch rig', (with which soft plastic shads and eels can also be used) invented by Frenchman Albert Drachkovitch, which comprises a lightweight,

V-shaped sprung wire stem inserted down the dead bait's throat, to which at the top clip is attached a ball weight of between (depending upon depth, casting distance and current force) 4-12 grams.

Also attached to the clip is around six inches of stiff copper wire, which is threaded once through the bleak's slim body at the shoulder, and then wound firmly around the body. Two single trebles joined to wire or tough braid, one short and one long, are pushed

Left: Tip 1

Above: Tip 2

Far Right: Tip 3

colour of strong tea. That's when! This enigmatic predator, with its huge 'glassy' eyes is superbly equipped for hunting out its preferred prey of small shoal fishes like roach, rudd, dace, gudgeon, bleak and skimmer bream, both during the hours of darkness and when flooded rivers offer minimal visibility. Exactly the kind of conditions you would not fancy for pike fishing, are exactly what zander prefer.

4 During the warmer months, at dusk and at dawn (again, during low light levels) are prime times for finding zander in a feeding mood, and of course, at any time during the hours of darkness, especially during mild spells of winter weather.

into the fish's flank and tail root on opposing sides, to ensure a hook-up from whatever angle the zander grabs hold. Expect those juddery, snappy 'takes' from zander both on the drop, as the bait 'flutters', and whilst on the jerk, by working the bait constantly with your rod tip. Strike at anything 'positive'.

3 When is the best time to go zander fishing in the British Isles? When following a couple of weeks of intermittent, often heavy rain, the rivers are well up and running the

5 Whether you offer lures or use dead or live baits to tempt zander, you will catch infinitely more fish by striking instantly, certainly 'earlier' rather than later. As this predator is 'ultra sensitive' to resistance, the worst course of action is to allow several yards of line to evaporate from the spool as you might prior to hitting a run from other predators such as eels, pike and catfish. The further it runs off with your bait, the more

resistance it will feel, especially if it runs off at right angles to the ledger bomb (zander living in Fenland Drains have no option but to run along the drain) and eventually it will either eject the bait, or you will be unable to straighten the line out in order to set the hooks.

6 'Twitching' a small dead bait back just above bottom after waiting some time without a run, is often the 'trigger' to catching this finicky feeder. So above your wire trace and two-treble hook set up, with a large bead on the reel line in between, use a 'bomb link-ledger' which ensures the bait won't foul bottom during the 'twitch' back. Eight inches of stiff rig tubing is threaded over 15lbs mono to form the link, with a bomb tied at one end and a ¼inch diameter ring and buoyant rig foam body at the top.

This set up can be used in conjunction with a ledger bobbin, and the bait left static for a minute or two between bouts of 'twitching'. It will certainly keep you active alternating between two or three rods.

7 To catch zander on small live and dead baits choose roach, rudd or dace, (gudgeon work well

Far Right: Tip 14

too) between 3 and 5 inches long. Every so often a big zander will wolf down an 8 inch skimmer bream intended for pike, as they will the occasional sea dead bait, like a smelt or a herring. But generally speaking zander are not receptive to sea baits, nor anything over large. What they do seem to home into however and often with surprising speed, are small, indigenous, freshwater fish freshly killed that have been 'stabbed' a few times with a sharp knife, immediately prior to casting, which allows those attractive 'juices' to permeate quickly downstream with the current. Try it and see.

8 While there is just the 'one' species called zander in European rivers and lakes, two extremely similar species, sauger, and the larger, walleye, are found in North American freshwater. A small number of North American walleye, were in fact introduced into The Fens way back in 1925, long before the controversial stock of 97 zander were introduced into the Great Ouse Relief Channel in 1963.

9 There is actually a British record 'walleye' that weighed 11lb 12oz, caught from the River Delph by Mr F Adams in 1934, although as early as the 1870s, European zander were being brought across the Channel by boat to stock The Duke of Bedford's Lakes at Woburn. And there were numerous subsequent stockings of both European and home-grown zander into various southern waters during the 1920s, 1940s and the 1950s.

10 You'll catch far more zander, and enjoy their scrap much more, by not simply using the same tackle you do for pike. And it's all down to reducing 'drag' and 'resistance' to a biting fish. An 8lbs reel line matched to an Avon-type rod for instance is quite adequate, (double figure barbel come out on the same strength, and such fish fight far harder than zander) or 10lbs test at the most.

11 The same goes for trace wire and hooks. A 'soft', fine, multi-strand wire of around 15lb test twisted onto a size 10 swivel, is more than adequate yet strong enough for pike should one (as they regularly do) pick up your bait intended for zander. And with hooks, a duo of semi-barbed fine wire, size 10 fits the bill admirably.

12 If ledgering small live or dead baits for zander and the mono 'bomb' link which slides on the line above your wire trace repeatedly 'twists' around the wire, which it sometimes manages to do with surprising ease, then here's how to alleviate the problem. For starters, make the 4-6 inch bomb link from 'stiff' 20lbs test mono. And secondly, incorporate a 10 inch section of mono (same as reel line) above your wire trace, the top swivel of which, (with a bead in between) the swivel of your 'bomb' link rests against. Tangles will then not happen.

13 When striking into zander be gentle. Simply wind down to

take up any slack and slowly pull the rod back and upwards whilst reeling. Most times the hooks actually find purchase when the zander opens its mouth and shakes its head from side to side in order to eject the bait, just like a perch. And a heavy strike at this time will only pull out the trebles, especially from lightly hooked fish.

14 Learn to pull into mere one and two inch 'lifts' or 'drops' of the ledger bobbin when ledgering with small dead baits in clear water conditions and when zander are being particularly finicky. Sometimes, any stronger indications simply will not happen before the bait is ejected.

15 Short, two to three inch sections of ½ - ¾ inch diameter eel or lamprey ledgered static on the bottom, can prove 'magical', and at such times zander will show a complete and distinct preference for them to all other dead baits.

16 In rivers and slow moving drains, trotting live bait downstream beneath a sliding float rig, into areas of low light such as beneath road and rail bridges can really prove productive. Such areas are inevitably quite deep (due to the excavation

Far Left: Tip 17

work and piling when constructing the bridge) and are usually prime zander 'hot spots'. So plumb each run accurately and set the float to present the bait (a gudgeon or small roach, etc) two feet above bottom, with a swan shot pinched onto the wire trace just below the swivel to keep it down, and wind quickly down to pull into a fish immediately the float disappears. Wait too long and it will feel resistance and eject the bait.

17 On some of our larger rivers where zander have become well established, such as the River Severn, the Warwickshire Avon or the River Nene, locating them by going afloat and using a fish finder, can provide superlative daytime sport with artificial lures, particularly 'rubber shads'. Generally, the smaller sizes are best, when worked in a 'jigging', up and down action once bottom has been found.

18 By far the best selection of synthetic rubber shad-like artificials is marketed through 'Storm'. Available in just about every shape size and colour, many of these decidedly 'real to the touch' soft rubber and plastic, internally-leaded artificials are fitted with just a large single hook protruding from behind the dorsal fin. These models are ideal for working in and around weedy and snaggy areas without catching up.

19 Other types of rubber and plastic bodied lures, in addition to the large single also come fitted with a small treble protruding from the pelvic fins, and they all attract and catch zander 'big time' due to the vibratory, throbbing action from either curl or block tails. Some even have holographic flash foil, scented bodies impregnated with various oils. All have life-like swimming actions, and some are actually designed to be trolled. Try them all. But stick to the smaller 'zander' sized models of between 9-14cm in length.

20 An ideal combo for working 'rubbers', is an eight-nine foot, tip-actioned spinning rod coupled to a small fixed spool reel or baby multiplier, loaded with 12-18lbs test braid, for maximum sensitivity. Hits are often extremely gentle 'taps' and 'judders' of the rod tip, and you need to strike into any potential hit, no matter how slight the pull. Obviously, where pike are regularly encountered a short, (5-6 inch) but soft, multi-strand wire trace is imperative.

The pictures in this book were provided courtesy of the following:

JOHN WILSON

Cover Design & Updates: ALEX YOUNG

Published under licence from: G2 ENTERTAINMENT LTD

Publisher: JULES GAMMOND

Written by: JOHN WILSON